Choosing for Teens

Your Survival Guide to Navigating the Career Maze in Today's Fast-Changing World

Oscar Frank

© **Copyright 2023 - All rights reserved.**

The content contained within this book may not be reproduced, duplicated or transmitted without direct written permission from the author or the publisher.

Under no circumstances will any blame or legal responsibility be held against the publisher, or author, for any damages, reparation, or monetary loss due to the information contained within this book, either directly or indirectly.

Legal Notice:

This book is copyright protected. It is only for personal use. You cannot amend, distribute, sell, use, quote or paraphrase any part, or the content within this book, without the consent of the author or publisher.

Disclaimer Notice:

Please note the information contained within this document is for educational and entertainment purposes only. All effort has been executed to present accurate, up to date, reliable, complete information. No warranties of any kind are declared or implied. Readers acknowledge that the author is not engaged in the rendering of legal, financial, medical or professional advice. The content within this book has been derived from various sources. Please consult a licensed professional before attempting any techniques outlined in this book.

By reading this document, the reader agrees that under no circumstances is the author responsible for any losses, direct or indirect, that are incurred as a result of the use of the information contained within this document, including, but not limited to, errors, omissions, or inaccuracies.

Table of Contents

INTRODUCTION 1
   ABOUT OSCAR FRANK 4

CHAPTER 1: SURVEYING AND STRATEGIZING 5
   WHAT IS A *CAREER*? CAN IT BE *PLANNED*? 8
   THE FLUIDITY IN PLANNING A CAREER TODAY 9
   CONSIDERATIONS 10
   THE THREE-STEP APPROACH 11
      1. Ruminate 11
      2. Survey 11
      3. Scheme 13
   KEY POINTS 14

CHAPTER 2: RECONNOITERING 15
   TYPES OF EXPERIENCES 16
      Pre-Graduation Experience 17
      Post-Graduation Jobs 19
      Career Paths According to Sectors in the Market 21
   KEY POINTS 24

CHAPTER 3: PREPARING FOR BATTLE 27
   ONE TRUE PURPOSE 28
      Aptitude, Attitude, and Competition 31
   HOW CAN EDUCATION HELP? 33
      Financial Planning 35
   WHAT IF I DON'T KNOW MY GOAL YET? 36
   KEY POINTS 37

CHAPTER 4: CONSULTING YOUR ADVISORS 39
   CAREER CLUSTERS 41
   BUILDING CONVERSATIONS ON CAREER CHOICES—WHAT? WHY? WHO? 46
      Conversations on Careers Continued 48
   KEY POINTS 50

CHAPTER 5: TRAINING 51

THE TIERS OF THE EDUCATION SYSTEM 52
   When Do I Start Thinking of a Career? 55
EARLY HIGH SCHOOL: THE FRESHMAN AND SOPHOMORE 55
LATE HIGH SCHOOL: THE JUNIOR AND SENIOR 57
BEYOND HIGH SCHOOL 58
   Types of Institutions 61
KEY POINTS 62

CHAPTER 6: CHARTING YOUR COURSE(S) 65

   Classes That Will Aid College 68
   Higher Level Courses 69
   How Do I Study? 71
TESTING WATERS 73
SEARCHING FOR A COLLEGE 74
   Some Resources 74
   Online Resources 74
   Books 75
   Facing Interviews 76
   The Questions 77
   Preparing for Ivy League 78
KEY POINTS 79

CHAPTER 7: DIVING INTO COMBAT 81

JOB HUNTING AND PREPARATION 82
   Doing What Is Right vs. What Makes You Happy 82
   Where Do I Start? 83
   Understanding the Industry 83
   Expectations vs. Reality 84
   Understanding the Requirements to Get Selected 84
   Resume 85
   The Whole Gamut of Communication Skills 86
NEGOTIATING EMPLOYER AND EMPLOYEE EXPECTATIONS 89
THE LADDER OF SUCCESS 90
KEY POINTS 91

CHAPTER 8: BECOMING A FREELANCER 93

   Considerations to be Self–Employed 96
   Types of Self-Employment 98
KEY POINTS 101

CHAPTER 9: MODERNIZING YOUR ARSENAL 103
- SOME RECENT TRENDS 104
- ONLINE MARKETPLACES AND HOW THEY PAY 106
- A STEP-BY-STEP GUIDE 109
- KEY POINTS 111

CHAPTER 10: VANQUISHING VULNERABILITY 113
- INTROSPECTION 114
  - *Personal Introspection* 115
  - *Personal to Professional Branding* 117
  - *Some Common Barriers and Coping Strategies* 118
  - *Core Values* 121
- A FEW RESOURCES 122
  - *Websites and e–Resources* 123
- KEY POINTS 123

CONCLUSION 125

REFERENCES 127
- IMAGE REFERENCES 133

Introduction

A very dear friend I know from India changed her career track at least three times. Now, before you jump the gun, let me clarify. She is one of the smartest people I know; she was top of her class, getting straight A's in every subject, and she adhered to every last word the teachers said. In high school, nobody was really surprised when she took up Science as her major. If not a doctor, everyone assumed she would at least become an engineer. She was one of the top students in her final exams. There's no real surprise there, either.

She did shock people, though. She never even sat for the engineering or medical entrance exams that most of her peers were sweating over. In India, there are only two professions for the really smart: medicine or engineering, the latter preferably from an IIT. That is at least what most parents and families goad children into, at any rate. She had found an alternative career path, or so she thought.

She worked hard and passed the Chartered Accountancy entrance exam (the Indian equivalent of the CPA in the United States or the ACCA in the United Kingdom) on the first try. People were skeptical but still encouraged. I mean, a CA earns more than many doctors and engineers in India. So, people were still impressed. But seven months or more into the course, she decided that this simply was not the field for her. It wasn't just the grind of the syllabus, which she could have surmounted, or even the mandatory and sometimes long hours of articles the course required that consumed her with anxiety. It was simply that she had no real love for what she was doing and was tired of trying to pretend that her heart was in it. So, she quit (yes, the taboo word) after giving it one last shot for two more months. Truth be told, she was a bit of a failure in everybody's eyes, including hers.

She then did the unthinkable. She enrolled in English literature. Now in India, taking up a course in the Arts stream is believed to be tantamount to committing suicide for your career. That's what people told her, sneeringly. It is only the people who aren't smart enough for Science or Commerce—the *dregs* of the academic system—who end up in Arts! To say that these statements did not affect her at all would be a lie. At one point or another, it was what all students heard and internalized. She worked hard though, and she completed her three-year bachelor's course in English with a university rank. She then cleared the entrance test for an MA course in English at one of the best universities in the country, and enrolled there with a scholarship she'd won. The jeering hadn't died down, but it had become subdued. She went on to become the university gold medalist in her course. This was a different city and a different university, and she still managed to retain her top position.

She became a lecturer at a college. If not the highest-paying job, it certainly had a respectable reputation. She changed cities, taught at top colleges in three big cities, and completed an MPhil in English while continuing to work. It seemed that all she had to do now was get a PhD for her career to reach its zenith. But she wasn't done.

Just as people thought that she had *settled down*, she resigned after her maternity break and took a break (a second taboo word). People were, of course, very concerned about her career at a time when she wanted to focus on her baby. She heard statements like, "But when will you rejoin work?" "Isn't a steady income more important now, that you will have more financial obligations coming up?"

After a year and a half, she got back to work—not teaching, though. She decided that she wanted to become a content

2

writer. She took up a full-time job with a small firm while also simultaneously focusing on gathering a clientele of her own. She did every kind of writing task that came her way. Her clients had different needs. Some wanted blogs or articles or academic textbooks or ghostwritten books; she did them all. But that is not what I want you to focus on. She had a degree in the arts and had taken a few detours in her academic and career paths, but she was earning as much as many of her friends who had followed the traditional path of engineering or medicine. *Take that, societal norms!*

What was more was that she fully enjoyed what she was doing and had the flexibility of working from home, something that had become a priority for her. The fact that she had high school-level comprehension of Science, Commerce, Math, and a good grasp of English helped her weave content in a wide array of areas that her clients appreciated. That she had been part of so many fields and knew a little about finance, science, and the arts made a difference in the way she articulated and presented her ideas.

You may wonder what the point of this story is. Am I suggesting that you should switch careers multiple times to find happiness and success? Most emphatically not! What I am instead going to tell you is that there is no fixed route to finding success in a career. *Choosing a Career Path for Teens* will guide you through the options you have, arm you with plenty of resources from which you can gather knowledge, and help you make informed choices. You must admit that this is better than jumping into something blindly, only based on hearsay, your own hunch, or other people's opinions. This book will also help you find your voice and stance so that you have the skill, confidence, and ability to make the right moves at the right time, should you ever find yourself in that position. Who wants to get stuck in a job forever simply because they lack what it takes to be adaptable? The next section will tell you why the author of this book is the best qualified to give you these tips.

About Oscar Frank

Oscar Frank founded his successful career on having a quality foundation in everything he did. Knowing that this begins during one's teen years, Oscar uses his experience and challenges from his personal life while growing up to create self-help books for teens, preparing them for college and life thereafter. He loves a good story, and the book will have as its real-life framework examples of success from all around the globe and lessons he'd like his readers to take away.

Oscar, a man with an intense, sometimes strangely wry sense of humor, infuses his writing with his wit and energy. The last thing he wants is for readers to grow bored of his books and step away without absorbing critical information that might mean the fine line between success and failure for them (his readers, not his books, or perhaps both? Ha Ha!). Oscar's passion stems from wanting to help people live their best lives.

Now that we know a little about what this book is about and who wrote it, what are you waiting for? Let's plunge right in!

1
Surveying and Strategizing

Some are born great, some achieve greatness, and some have greatness thrust upon them. –William Shakespeare

I first read the quote above when I read Charles Lamb's *Shakespeare for Children* when I was about 12 or 13 years old. It has stuck with me ever since, you could say. The quote relates to how people find greatness. There are those who are thrust into the limelight—say, for instance, a prince or princess who is an heir to a throne. Their birth alone is a passport to their fame. Then there are those who achieve greatness by dint of their actions or work. Think of most actors, writers, or politicians, who rise in popularity by working hard towards their goals. There is a third group of people who unwittingly stumble upon fame. They never asked for it and didn't do anything very extraordinary. Call it a chance, good fortune, or whatever you will, but they are noticed and end up getting caught in the spotlight. Think of the many memes and videos that go viral today—the creators of which were just having some fun, never assuming that their posts would get so many likes and shares. You'll get the idea.

Now, the same quote could be true about the careers we are given, the jobs we choose, or the jobs we fall into by accident. Many are born into careers that are picked for them by their parents, teachers, or peers. Their potential and aptitude are discovered, measured, and fixed by others, and they are asked to register for a course, write a test, or do this or that, and they just keep building on every step forward. And hey! No judgment. Some of them do quite well in their lives, which were planned and plotted by forces outside them.

There are quite a lot of people who find paths for themselves. They realize things they are passionate about, recognize a specific goal they want to achieve, and work towards that. There are sometimes missteps and failures, but these people believe in themselves and try and try again till they succeed or are recognized. These people are looked up to because they surmount every obstacle in their way by dint of their faith in themselves. This is not an easy road, but those who have traveled it will tell you that success achieved thus will taste like manna fit for the Gods.

The third group of people are those who fall into careers or jobs quite by accident. Think of the investment banker who ends up an actor or the doctor who turns to law. You must have come across at least a few such stories wherein a chance event, a person, or a new hobby ignites true passion, a calling, in a person. They then decide to set aside their earlier goals, put them on the backburner or as a backup plan, and then devote their talents to this new-found passion until they make it or give up tired.

Which of the above categories do you most fit into? Do you want to be guided by the hand into a profession? Do you want to discover and make your own career? Do you want to be jolted into a vocation? The answer to these questions will depend a lot on your personality, the people you are most in touch with, and the situations that you encounter.

Let me tell you a story here. A 10-year-old boy named Henry Burner had to complete a project on trading homemade items at his school in Washington in 2013. When his mother suggested a traditional baked cookie stall, he rejected the idea, telling her that the market would be *totally oversaturated*. He then came up with the unique idea of selling pinback buttons to his classmates. Being dyslexic and successful at school was not something that came naturally to Henry. So, when his merchandise did well, everyone was ecstatic. With the encouragement that he got, he started selling his wares at the local farmer's markets and then via his website, Buttonsmith Inc., and Amazon as well. With the greater reach that allowed him, he added more products to his catalog, which now had buttons, lanyards, badges, swappable head badge reels, and several other products. Slowly, the home-based manufacturing unit moved out of their home and opened a small shop front. Henry also ensured that customizable products were made available to online shoppers. Today, his company has 12 employees and has made over ten million dollars in total revenue. His products are available on many other popular online stores, such as Etsy and Shopify (About Us, 2023).

So where would you place this story? Henry was certainly not born to fame, and neither was button-making a natural profession he grew up into. A series of events and people were instrumental in Henry's growth story, and he made the most of the situations that presented themselves to him.

If you are asking yourself now, *What can I do to become a Henry Burner?* I'd tell you point-blank that you are asking yourself the wrong thing. The question you must be asking yourself here is:

How can I become _____ (insert your full name here)*?*

The next couple of sections will bring you closer to formulating an answer to this question in terms of:

1. Can I *plan* a career?

2. How will I know if I'm any good at it?

3. What are my options, and how do I sift through them?

Let me put the answers to these questions in perspective for you.

What Is a *Career*? Can It Be *Planned*?

Let's just start at the very beginning. The Merriam-Webster dictionary defines *career* in two ways: It is "a profession for which one trains, and which is undertaken as a permanent calling." It is also "a field for or pursuit of consecutive progressive achievement, especially in public, professional, or business life." Taking both senses of the term together, a career is simply a chosen profession or job in which you would want to succeed and grow one step at a time. So now that we have some idea of what the word means, the next logical question is, "What does it mean for me?"

As a teenager, you already have your hands full with schoolwork, homework, extracurricular activities, sports, hobbies, an expanding social circle, perhaps the possibility of romance (yes, I have been there too, you know), and so many other things. The world is full of possibilities, and the thought of narrowing it down to just one, two, or even three will lie somewhere on the spectrum, from daunting to boring. You might find it confusing to know what you really want.

Let me tell you here that this confusion is not just natural but also desirable. If your mind were stuck on a single track, there would be no confusion. You'd just go ahead on the path paved for you, and the hardest task would be to simply stick to it. But that's not what a majority of us are aiming for. Most of us need to know what we aren't good at, are okay–good at, and excel at.

I am not suggesting that you should already have a set plan or even that you should form one by the end of this book. But you are good to go if you have two qualities:

1. An insatiable curiosity to know more about everyone and everything around you.

2. The ability to keep adapting yourself to the changing environment around you.

Now don't worry! It is possible to imbibe these qualities over time with the right resources, and I will share with you what you can do in your own way to stay tuned to the right career choice.

The Fluidity in Planning a Career Today

Even ten years ago, there were not as many job opportunities as there are today. With the internet and technology advancing every single day, the job market has virtually and exponentially exploded. In modern parlance, one no longer associates a *job* as one that entails a person walking out in the morning with a satchel and doing a nine-to-five shift. There are so many types of jobs and work models available that it has become much more flexible. The startup culture has also opened up more entrepreneurial avenues for people all over the globe. The pandemic made us sit up and notice the importance of working from home or even putting in place a hybrid culture that would give employees the flexibility of scheduling their work either in or outside of the office.

A couple of months ago, I read about the concept of a *virtual assistant*. To me, this term brought up memories of Jarvis from the *Ironman* franchise. (I have been something of a huge Marvel fan, so you'll pardon this obvious connection I made.) As it turns out, a virtual assistant is something much simpler than what I had in mind. Imagine a personal secretary who is in charge of sorting out your day, arranging, scheduling, or reminding you of your appointments and meetings, probably taking care of the employee payroll, and performing a variety of other job functions. Now imagine that your assistant does all this and more for you while working remotely for you. And why not? All of these tasks, which necessitated a person's presence in the office earlier, can be done via mail, online calendars, phone calls, or other online platforms—including handling payroll! What is the need for a secretary to be present in the office today? And this is just one of the hundreds of thousands of such opportunities that are beginning to be identified and tapped! Exciting times ahead? You bet!

Considerations

So, do you just jump headlong into the sea of vast possibilities and hope that you strike gold before long? Sure, that's one way of doing it, and I'd be lying if I said that nobody had made the cut that way. However, there is, I believe, a better way of doing things. Especially if you are one of those people who are anxious about their future and want to explore avenues but also have a blueprint of personal targets to achieve, then I would advise at least three steps before you head out into the big bad world. I will be addressing all three of these throughout this book, but let me sum them up for you here, so you have an idea of how this book will unfold for you.

The Three-Step Approach

1. Ruminate

Sometimes I do like to show off my vocabulary.

Ruminate is basically a fancier word for "think," except that it doesn't just mean to think. It means going over the things you have done, the people you have met, the conversations you have had, and the experiences that you have been a part of. Now reflect on those memories that have genuinely made you happy. What is the one thing that keeps you going? This could be a subject you study at school, an interest, a hobby, or something that you don't even deem very valuable at the moment, like reading, stitching, being part of a sport, journaling, or painting. These current interests you have will do for a start.

Now it is important to remember that these are neither *all* your options nor are you stuck with *only* these simply because you happened to make a list now. This list can be expanded to include more hobbies as you find them or scaled down as you find that some interests no longer sustain your passion.

2. Survey

Exploration is a very important part of a career hunt. Once you have even a small list of hobbies and interests in hand, you can start searching for ways in which other people have built on similar strengths. Think of all the ways in which your hobby can become an opportunity.

For this, you can start by paying your local library a visit to read up on specific areas of interest or scanning the jobs readily available in the area. Focus on the skills and expertise that acquiring and holding down such a job would require. Keep a journal of all that you read, including the resources (websites, books, articles, video links, or podcasts) from where you got the information. This will lead to the third step I'll be coming to shortly.

Secondly, talk to people who have been in a job that you think you might enjoy. These people will give you the inside scoop on the day-in and day-out grind. This will, in turn, give you a more realistic picture of whether you will fit in.

Thirdly, take action and enroll yourself in anything that you think might give you more insight into the subject—contests, courses, workshops, seminars, or conferences. This will also give you an idea of the competition out there and the chance to measure your abilities against those of others who are interested in the same field.

Self-assessment is a related and invaluable tool when it comes to exploration. You have to have a realistic idea of your potential, and sometimes you may not be the best judge of that. It is essential to rely on your parents, teachers, peers, and other outsiders to sometimes give you their opinion of your ability. I'm not asking you to take every opinion at face value, but the average feedback that you get may not be very far from the truth. For instance, you may think you are a gifted dancer and may even work hard at your moves. Your best friend and sibling may be your greatest cheerleaders. Your parents haven't exactly praised you as a good dancer. You have never won any of the inter-school competitions despite participating five years in a row. Some of your other classmates jeer at your dancing; your teacher has once or twice gently tried to dissuade you from trying out for the school dance team. If you have taken all the feedback, collated it, and mulled it over, you will (hopefully) arrive at the logical conclusion that you are not, perhaps, the best dancer. This is not to say you don't have to dance at all in your life, but turning it into a professional career may not be the wisest move for you personally.

3. Scheme

Planning is almost as important as surveying. This is the stage that will ultimately decide how you are going to put all the information that you have gathered to good use. You may have to seek the help of a career counselor as you decide what course or stream you want to take and whether you would be happy in it or even be able to handle all the components of your choice. For instance, you may like chemistry but hate math. You might want to rethink a course in chemical engineering if you feel that the math that is a mandatory part would be too advanced for you to cope with.

How you will take on the financial obligation of this course is another consideration that you will have to work out with your parents. You may have to rely on scholarships or loans if you want to finance the entire course yourself.

I would also like to make a brief mention of the manifold (*hey, there's another fancy word*) career and personality assessment tests that are available online. Though you can take them and get a few ideas, I would ask you to take the results with a pinch of salt. Many online tests and games have their own agendas or are too generalized to give you a complete or detailed picture. However, the importance of your specific personality and behavioral traits that will play into the career you choose is another aspect that this book will address.

Let me address one last point before I conclude this chapter. Rumination, survey, and scheming may look like three hierarchical steps to choosing a career, but they are more of an evolutionary cycle. At times, your survey may lead you back to rumination and a new scheme. Sometimes a scheme that you thought foolproof will have to be discarded, and you'll have more surveying and ruminating about doing. Be open to change.

Key Points

Choosing the best career for yourself is based on three primary steps that you can undertake:

1. Ruminate on your strengths and weaknesses.

2. Survey the choices you have that will suit you.

3. Scheme ahead.

The next section will focus on how you can evaluate your options, which will help you in your quest.

2

Reconnoitering

Begin somewhere. You cannot build a reputation on what you intend to do.
—Liz Smith

Abasiama Idaresit returned to Nigeria in 2009 after his course at the London School of Economics. He had a brain wave. He wanted to start a digital marketing company at a time when Nigerians had never even heard of the term. He started Wild Fusion and launched it in 2010. There was only one problem. There were no investors, and for eight months, he struggled, trying to keep his venture afloat. Hope dawned in the form of Baby M, a company that sold products targeted at newborns and their caregivers. At the time they approached Abasiama, their agents used to wander from house to house trying to sell these products, and they could hardly make profits over the costs involved in marketing their products. He met with the representatives of Baby M and told them that he would return their investment if he couldn't improve their sales through his platform. They gave him $250 as the initial investment. Using this, Abasiama worked hard, and at the end of the year, he increased Baby M's revenue a hundred times! From $1,000, Baby M's monthly sales touched $100,000. Google took up Wild Fusion as one of its case studies for digital marketing in Africa and even made Wild Fusion one of its first Google Adwords certified partners in Nigeria. In the years to follow, Wild Fusion would make millions more and collaborate with high-profile clients like Vodacom, Unilever, and Diamond Bank without additional investments (BellaNaija, 2017).

Abasiama had to spend a good eight months searching for the right customer, one who would be desperate enough to require his service and also truly benefit from it. This is why the results he achieved were spectacular. One of the biggest problems that you could encounter as you start taking stock of your choices will be how and where to start. No book or resource will be able to give you a comprehensive list of all the employment options in the world or of the experiences that you could master. This research will be made easier if you segregate the types of career paths based on qualifications and the market sectors. So let's first set up a concrete *way* of narrowing down your search, and then this may give you ideas to explore further.

Types of Experiences

One of the best parts of living in the 21st century is the fact that many job descriptions no longer insist on a formal degree or qualification. If you have the right attitude of being proactive, learning on the go, and making quick but accurate decisions, people are willing to hire you. There are also more technical jobs that will require a minimum degree or a certain specialization.

The conundrum of whether the chicken came from the egg or the egg from the chicken is a cliche by now. But similar to that, one of the primary things you will have to decide is whether you want to take up a job before you earn a degree and perhaps later work towards a more solid qualification or whether you want to complete your education once and for all before you jump into the job market. Answering this will simplify the next couple of steps that you need to take. This question will also come with financial considerations, such as whether earning while still a student is important to you or not. Once you make up your mind, this search will get easier. Let us now quickly look at what kinds of experiences you can look at pre- and post-graduation and also at choices such as working full- or part-time.

Pre-Graduation Experience

I will eventually get a job when I am an adult; why do I need to be stuck in this rut now? Guess who asked this question when in their teens? That was me, trying to sit out my summer job during my school vacation. I was told in return that I could wait till I was an adult to enjoy some of the benefits that I was enjoying at home then, like free food and accommodation. This, of course, made me rethink and recant my ideals a bit.

Several of the pre-graduation experiences are training periods for which you will need basic skills such as good communication, listening, and time management. For starters, these pre-employment options will provide you with the primary skill sets that you will carry forward to any other job in the future. Irrespective of the time you decide to spend in your first couple of roles, focus on what you can bring to the table and what you can learn while being there.

I know, I know what the Joker from *The Dark Knight* said: *If you're good at something, never do it for free.* And I agree 100% with him! However, I've already calculated this defense into the argument I've framed. The quote I started this chapter with will stand as a testament to this. I outthought you, didn't I?

Some of the jobs may not pay you yet, but they will provide you with concrete experience and skill sets in the area of your interest. For example:

- Apprenticeship: Normally of a slightly longer duration than internships and other types of experiences, apprenticeships will allow you to work under a guide or mentor in an area of your interest. You may get a weekly or monthly stipend during this period. Once you complete the tasks required of you, you will gain either a certification, a qualification, or particular skills that will help you land a job in the same area.

- Externships: These last for about a week and mainly consist of you observing people in a professional setting at their jobs so that you have an insider's perspective about what you would have to do if you worked there. You may also be delegated some tasks, attend meetings, and learn about the job functions associated with the role. These are generally unpaid.

- Internship: Some internships pay you, while others will only give you a letter of experience or recommendation. However, in an internship, you will get the chance to work hands-on on projects related to your area of interest or expertise. It is also over a couple of months generally, which means that they offer you the chance to weigh whether you would make a good fit for this career.

- Job shadowing: This is usually a day's experience of watching professionals in their line of work and asking them questions regarding their daily activities while at work. Though this may provide you with a basic idea of the job role, it may not be enough for you to make a decision about whether you would be a good fit.

- Service learning: These are real-time opportunities for you to learn about social problems like poverty, homelessness, or illiteracy and what you can do to solve them. These opportunities are crafted to help both the individual and the community. Like volunteering, these may not provide you with an income, though.

- Student Teaching: These are chances for students to teach others and thereby improve their learning and communication skills. Being part of certain schools, colleges, or universities that have tie-ups with other institutions, you can sign up to teach other students with or without pay. Classes will be over a predefined period of time, and you will get an experience letter and credentials.

- Undergraduate Research: Schools or colleges may recruit you with a stipend to help with research projects that are currently happening there. This would be a great way of working in the field and understanding your keenness for the subject while gathering practical learning experience.

- Volunteering: These are unpaid learning opportunities where you can work on social causes that motivate you. You could work with a pet shelter if you care about the safety of stray animals. You can work with a relevant NGO if you care about promoting gender equality and so on.

Post-Graduation Jobs

Selecting a course and a college where you get guidance before and after you finish your degree is very important. Several of the more technical courses that you enroll in will have a combination of internships or apprenticeships tailored into them so that by the time you finish your course, you will already have the experience to show on your resume. When you complete your course, you will also have career placement opportunities or drives where companies will come to your college, search for, and hire candidates they think will make a good fit. If you happen to be a part of an institution or course where such opportunities are limited, you will have to seek the help of a career counselor or coach to find out the options available to you. You can also use the internet and ask your teachers to get a more concrete idea about the employability of that course.

I came across an interesting initiative by the UK government to list most of the available career choices alphabetically to guide students who may feel lost. The *Career A-Z* list page of the NiDirect website, sponsored by the UK government, lists almost every career choice that one can think of, along with the certifications, qualifications, and experience that would be necessary to become a part of them. There are similar government-sponsored web pages available for young adults in the US and Australia. Of course, the criteria for some jobs might be country-specific, but the list will help you identify niche jobs that you may not yet have thought of or even know existed.

We know that time is of the essence, and learning to manage it is the fundamental aspect of adulting—something even most adults suck at. Now that we have looked at some of the keyways in which one can gather experience let us look at two ways in which you can work to make the most of the time available to you:

- Part-time: Any work that you do around another full-time occupation or your regular school hours would be part-time work. This would give you an additional source of income and equip you with the skills you need in your workplace as you work towards whatever is a top priority for you.

- Full-time: Full-time work options are those that require your presence or dedication from nine-to-five jobs or thereabouts on the days on which you are employed. Taking up such a job would mean that you would have to enroll in a part-time course or opt for distance education. Any other job or interest would have to be slotted around your regular work schedule.

In the next segment, we shall sort jobs by segments, which will help you for quick reference.

Career Paths According to Sectors in the Market

The Beatles unwittingly summed up adulting when they sang, "It's been a hard day's night, and I've been working like a dog." But perhaps searching for the ideal job needn't be as soul-wearying. Here we shall try to create a segment-based assortment of professions, which will help you quickly reference the type of job that you seek.

To reiterate, it would be near impossible to give an A–Z list of professions, but this is as good a way to start as any:

- Corporate: These are employee positions within large private companies or organizations, some of which may even have an international presence. Your role will depend on your experience and qualifications. Some features of corporate offices will be a more structured employee hierarchy, formal attire and codes of conduct, and regular working hours. If you are working at a local Starbucks Café as a store operations agent or manager, it may not count as corporate experience. But if you work at their headquarters or one of their centralized offices, handling supplies, procurement, or HR, it will most likely be a corporate role.

- Government: The government of each country will have several departments under its purview. When you are employed by the government, there could be a lot of perks and benefits to your job—including better job security, which may compensate for the slightly lower wages. However, some government jobs may also entail more rigorous tests and interviews to assess whether you would be compatible with the service segment, i.e., serving the people of your country.

- Project-based: When a company hires you not as a full-time employee but rather as part of an ongoing project for a certain duration, it is called a "project-based role." If they like your work, the company may decide to prolong your contract and hire you for other similar contracts or onboard you for a more permanent job. But there is no guarantee of this.

- Self-employed: How does the idea of working for yourself sound, as opposed to being micromanaged by a grumpy taskmaster, most likely with a permanent scowl? This may mean that you sell a product or service to customers that you find. With access to smartphones and laptops, it is relatively easy to find a market for your talents, whether you are an app developer, baker, blogger, interior designer, or writer. It may sound fancy, but it also means that you are your own boss, with all the responsibilities and freedoms that accompany it. After all, "With great power comes great responsibility" (Spider-Man).

- Own a startup: A startup is a venture or company that you finance, establish, and run. This is more complex than selling a product or service online, though this may be a part of your entrepreneurial journey. With a startup, you are your own boss (Woohoo! Get those world's best boss mugs out!), but you have to find the right funding resources, legally register your company, and put in the systems and procedures required for the day-to-day operations of the company. Later on, as your company expands, you'll have to identify talent and hire the right people for the right roles. It can be very exciting, though very stressful as well.

- Digital-based: As I said before, digital jobs are the present and future of the economy. Consider an illustrator who had to draw by hand, make a physical portfolio of his talent, and move from publisher to publisher with it for a job. Today most illustrators can complete their job at home (the comfort of working in your pajamas, I tell you!), on their PCs or tablets, create a digital portfolio, and mail it to prospective employers. Their job is not just restricted to publishing. There are allied fields, from web design to digital marketing or animation, where their talent would count. Even after getting hired, depending on company policies, they can continue to work from home. If you know how to harness technology to suit your needs, there is no end to the possibilities on offer. Just to quickly sum up, digital jobs can be further categorized in the following ways:

    o Digital Freelancer: A freelancer is one who is not tied to any one particular company. They offer their services and then establish links with companies or with individual clients to provide need-based services. For instance, a freelance writer will write documents, articles, blogs, or other content as per the client's requirements and be paid by the hour or per piece of work completed.

    o Digital marketing: This can be related to a wide array of areas, including website development and content creation, which may require additional skills like animation and web design. Digital marketing will also require copywriters who know the right verbiage to sell products and services. SEO knowledge to expand a website's visibility on the internet is another current and advantageous skill.

- o Full-time online services: If you are hired by a company to take care of their online customer services, and you have to deal with customer mail, chats, and possibly associated calls, this would count as a full-time online service. There are companies that have dedicated staff to take care of different aspects of their online services, and you may fit in with them.

Phew! That was a lot to take in. Are you still with me? It gets better from here, I promise. If you have the faintest idea of a career, I will encourage you to type in your interest on Google and see what others with similar skill sets are doing with their lives. You could also gradually start a profile on Linkedin, Glassdoor, or other professional platforms where you can interact with like-minded people and keep tabs on how much you can potentially earn by way of the career you have in mind. We will come back to this nefarious-sounding *earning potential* a little later on in the book as well.

Key Points

You can acquaint yourself with the necessities of your area of expertise in the following ways:

- You can sign up for pre-graduation experiences that will help you imbibe the skills necessary for any workplace.

- Check out post-graduation jobs that might give you relevant exposure to the job you seek.

- Explore part-time and full-time jobs, which will help you organize your time based on your priorities.

- Search for jobs based on the segments to which they belong and try to find out their pros and cons.

Let's next look at more concrete ways in which to prepare and empower yourself to meet the challenges of any career that you choose.

3

Preparing for Battle

Time spent in sharpening the axe may well be spared from swinging it. –
Josiah Strong

Every time I suspect a section of my book might read like a chapter out of a textbook, I feel anxious. I know most of you will share my distaste for textbooks. I remember that every time I used to pick up one of my school books with the intention of studying, I'd feel sweaty and clammy handed. I hope you appreciate the effort I'm making to liven this up for you. So here goes another inspirational story, this time all the way from Down Under.

This is the cue for you to clap and cheer.

In 2009, Melanie Perkins was only 22 years old when she was inspired to put together an app that could make people their own graphic designers. Most venture capitalists (i.e., people who invest in businesses in return for a stake in them) were not sold on the idea. Most graphic-design tools were tedious, slow, and required some amount of training to work with. There was no way that it could be simplified enough so that the average person could start using it for their everyday tasks. By the way, this was not the first time Melanie tried on an entrepreneurial hat. Six years ago, at the age of fourteen, she had been successfully selling hand-made scarves across stores in Perth!

Melanie and her partner, Cliff Obrecht, didn't give up. She caught the eye of businessman Bill Tai, who, though he didn't invest in her idea, was interested enough to introduce them to people he thought could play a role in their company. They kept honing her pitch and meeting more and more people, even going to Silicon Valley to meet investors. Finally, out of this endless preparation that Melanie and Cliff undertook were born what we today know as Canva, the app that lets you create posters and other social media presentations in a jiffy. Today, Canva is valued at $26 billion and has 60 million monthly users! (Williams, 2022).

The title of this chapter may sound too extreme. But it isn't far from the truth. Every year, there are millions of students who graduate from school and want to make it big—either via their chosen careers, professions, or businesses. And the sad fact of the matter is that the world cannot accommodate everyone who *wants* to do well. So what are the things that you must focus on to *stand apart* and, as mercenary as it may sound, to s*ell yourself*? This is just one of the aspects that we will look at in this chapter.

One True Purpose

Have you ever felt that you do things better when you shut out the noise? When I was a kid, studying in the evening proved to be a difficult matter at times. I would hear the sounds from the TV in the next room, the hum of the washing machine below the staircase, the door of the fridge opening and shutting as someone took a snack out of it, and even the water running in the sink in one of my siblings' bathrooms. And these were just the nearest sounds. Additionally, there would be the bark of a neighbor's dog or the horn of a passing car. Every sound seemed to cut into my resolve to focus on that book in my hands! (See why textbooks made me nervous?) It helped when I closed the door to my room and simply covered my ears with my headset to drown out the noise. I could focus on my reading or the essay I was writing much better then.

The distractions of the world are only going to grow. Now that the smartphone is almost always pinned to your side, just flicking through your social media news feed, taking a selfie, or playing a round or two of Candy Crush or PUBG (or whatever else is the most played game now) is going to get in the way of your research, studies, and ultimately your goal. Is there no respite? Yes, there is, but you are not going to like my answer. If your heart is set on something, you have to find the time, identify your distractors, and cut out their noise!

When you have found a purpose—and by that, I mean an interest, a hobby, or an area of study that you really enjoy—sometimes the only way to stay rooted is to stop all other distractions and focus on what you have to do a hundred percent. Now, I know this isn't possible for the entire length of the hours you are awake. What I mean is to dedicate a span of time *every day to that* one activity or pursuit. Say you decide to spend two hours in the evening learning advanced Algebra (I, for one, hated this subject—forgetting it has been one of the boons of completing college); you have to keep aside all other things like your phone, other books that you may want to read right then, or even the thought of the freshly baked cookies on the kitchen counter. Now, once you complete the two hours and the syllabus, you had intended to cover; you can go straight to the kitchen, pop one of those cookies into your mouth, and watch the latest episode of whichever series it was that you were so dying to watch just then. Do you know how your brain is wired to work? This is called the reward method. You work hard, but you also provide your system with a break, a reward for the hard work you just put in. Apart from this, how you work toward your goals will also set you apart.

Say you want to try out for a role in a play. What do you do? You read the play, its context, and more about the author and the characters. Now you choose a character and a setting that you feel you would be able to do justice to, learn their lines, and try to bring emotions to that character. Every day you practice those same lines in front of the mirror till you find yourself getting the voice, the posture, the accent, and the expressions, even to the rise of your brow, in line with how you think this character would have behaved. How can you improve on this? Initially, you may ask your parents, friends, or siblings to watch your performance and give you their opinion. But remember, none of them are actors. Their opinions can give you some general guidelines, but you want more detailed feedback. Well, you could watch videos of expert actors playing this particular role or enlist the help of your drama teacher, who may perhaps point out a nuance that your performance is missing. You could also check out the local drama troupes in your area and see if you can fix up an appointment with one of them so that you could learn a little more from their experience of acting, specifically of acting a character like the one you have chosen.

See what I am getting at? Sometimes it is not enough that you spend long hours on something. It also depends on *how* you spend this time. Practice is great, but practice with professional guidance can make the difference between a good performance and a *spectacular* performance.

We know that success stems from having fixed goals. But your determination to stick to those goals can go a long way in determining how successful you can become. Going back to the inspirational story at the beginning of this chapter, Melanie Perkins faced over a hundred rejections before she got her first investor in Canva. You have to explore every avenue at your disposal to see what more you can do to improve and showcase your talent.

Some questions that can probably help you with your search at this point are:

1. What can I study to make a career in _____?

2. Who are the experts in this field?

3. Is there a way in which I can talk to them before I make up my mind?

4. What will I earn if I become a/an _____?

5. Can I work from anywhere in the world as a/an _____?

Aptitude, Attitude, and Competition

You might've heard this story before, but bear with me. I heard this from a mentor I looked up to. There were two footwear salesmen who were recruited to sell shoes to the inhabitants of a faraway, remote island. This was a very long time ago, and the people of this island had never even worn sandals, to say the least, or shoes. They had never even heard of the concept of footwear.

The first salesman packed up his bags and left. He informed his employer by telegram:

"Situation bad. People here have not heard of shoes. No market possible."

The second salesman also wired his employer, and this is what it said:

"Excellent market to sell. Nobody here has heard of shoes. Send inventory."

Both the salesmen were top-selling agents of the company, and both of them had been provided the same opportunities and resources thus far. The first man, however, did not recognize the field before him. His despondence over people not even having heard of shoes sealed his attitude. The second man was thrilled that nobody on the island had ever owned footwear and interpreted this same situation as the best market and an opportunity to sell shoes to everyone.

Your aptitude will determine what you excel at and what you have a natural ability at. However, your attitude toward situations will be the ultimate judge of how well you do in life.

Having said this, it is equally important to understand that things will not turn around in a day. The second salesman is probably right in having identified a viable market full of potential. But he will have to work doubly hard to change the mindset of the people about wearing shoes. He will encounter questions like, "We haven't worn them for hundreds of years, so why must we start now?" He may also get less skeptical but more practical questions like, "Why should we spend our hard-earned money on shoes?" These are questions that the salesman will have to work into his selling strategy to convince people that wearing shoes will eventually save them money (probably on health bills related to the foot or back-related injuries) and will result overall in a happier, healthier lifestyle; all this without deriding the existing culture and lifestyle of the natives. Thus, the salesman will have to divide his market into smaller segments and try to conquer each market at a time, and he will have to hope that the benefits of the shoe–wearing will permeate into other segments gradually so that eventually, even the most hardcore skeptics might come to see the benefits of it. This, my dear reader, is no easy task!

To recapitulate, one needs specific skills (aptitude) and the right attitude. Now think of the competition. Just as our salesman is making some headway into the market and has captured, say, a fourth of it, he hears a competing salesman has just landed on shore. This new agent has shoes from a different company that is priced slightly cheaper. Our salesman can now decide to withdraw because he has covered the initial target set by his company. Or he can decide to stay and fight a new battle. This time, the natives are convinced about wearing shoes. Now he has to convince them why the shoes he sells are of better quality or more durable than those of his competitors. Now if the salesman himself is not convinced of this argument, he'll find that his customers will stray to the new agent. Thus, at this stage, it is important for the salesman to have not just complete faith in his selling abilities but also a concomitant faith in the product that he is selling. A slip-up in either of these will result in the loss of the goodwill that he has so carefully built up. If he feels that his shoes aren't as good as the new ones being sold, he will have to identify reasons why and write back to his company to check out a sleeker design, a better raw material, or ways in which the cost of production can be reduced.

What do we take away from this story? If you need to succeed, you have to gather the right skills with the aid of the right people around you. So take time to do your research and find the right opportunities for this. Secondly, a never-die attitude will enable you to recognize opportunities that others turn their backs on. This will give you a niche segment or unique area to work with, and we all know why pioneers have it tough but also do well. Thirdly, just as you think you have established yourself and are beginning to get complacent, there will be people who will want to do something similar to what you are doing. Identify them as your competitors and recognize ways in which you can stay ahead of them. Or, identify ways in which you can improve the product or service you are selling so you have the advantage of being the first as well as the best!

How Can Education Help?

"A little learning is a dangerous thing," said the renowned poet Alexander Pope. But, of course, he was talking about critics

bashing literary works based on their half-baked and ill-formed ideas. When it comes to any career choice (even entrepreneurship), the slightest educational edge you possess over others will only add to your resume's value and potential. Why? Well, let's look at a few reasons, shall we?

- Education gives you one of the best opportunities to sharpen your communication skills. Remember the pointless presentations, show-and-tell, group discussions, and debates that you did in class? This is where you will realize that they were not so pointless after all. Education provides you with the basic competencies for articulation, negotiation, and dialogue building.

- Remember the math exercises you spent your time pulling your hair over (I did, at any rate) or the essay that required you to research an endless variety of sources? Problem-solving is an intrinsic part of any course, and guess where else you'll need it? Yes, that's right, your whole life is going to be about making analytical decisions based on the data and the outcome you seek.

Education also provides you with the theoretical and practical experience necessary to tackle real-life challenges. Without knowing the theory you deem *boring*, it would be difficult to know where to apply what. Thus, you may not know it yet, but every one of those mundane lectures you attend is going to help you in some way. This would be especially applicable to those of you who have taken up Science or any other technical field of study.

Financial Planning

In the coming chapters, I will be talking more about consulting your parents about certain vital decisions that you make. But whenever you think of a course or degree, the following are some questions related to finances that must be tackled:

1. Can I manage my finances on my own?

2. To what extent will my parents be willing to help me out?

3. What are the other sources that I can check out? Government (called federal in the USA) loans vs. private student loans: what are the pros and cons of each?

4. What will be the duration of the loan?

5. What will be the rate of interest that I will pay on my loan?

6. If I take a loan, when does repayment start, and what will be the monthly amount I have to pay?

Remember that the terms of loans, like the interest rate, period, and monthly options you get, will vary according to your geographical location and the norms set by your country. So it is essential that you do thorough research and talk to others who have availed of student loans.

What If I Don't Know My Goal Yet?

If you are still with me so far, I know you must already be feeling a little stressed. But worry not! These are just pointers, and you still have plenty of time for the big decisions. You don't have to make up your mind or feel pressured to have a concrete plan of action. At this stage, as you are completing a basic level of education, it is more than enough if you have a list of options and are actively researching and talking to people about your plans.

It would be nice to plan a timeframe for when you would need to make a decision. Write down a checklist of expectations you have from yourself during this timeframe. The following is a sample, and you can modify it as per your needs:

1. My strengths:

2. My weaknesses:

3. Based on 1 and 2, a course in the _____ stream would suit me.

4. Colleges that I could consider, with pros and cons (distance, fees, and other criteria) for each.

    1. Option 1

    2. Option 2

    3. Option 3

5. Courses that I could consider in college, with pros and cons:

    1. Option 1

2. Option 2

3. Option 3

6. Financial requirements associated with each course.

Your final choice must be reflective of your financial and other considerations. Try not to select a course or a field that is so specialized that it would shut out other options for you. Instead, proceed with a general idea and narrow down your search as you proceed.

Key Points

To prepare yourself for the job market, you can try out the following:

- Make yourself more knowledgeable about the area of your interest and decide if you have the aptitude for it.

- Develop the right attitude to tackle what lies ahead.

- Understand that competition will exist and think of ways to stay ahead without letting it pull you under.

- Be convinced of the importance of completing a degree or formal education tied in as much as possible with your specific area or subjects.

- Don't worry too much about being clueless right now; gradually start working towards a concrete plan.

Coming up, are there practical ways to discuss a career plan with your parents and teachers and examine career clusters from which you can whittle down your options? Let us see the next chapter...

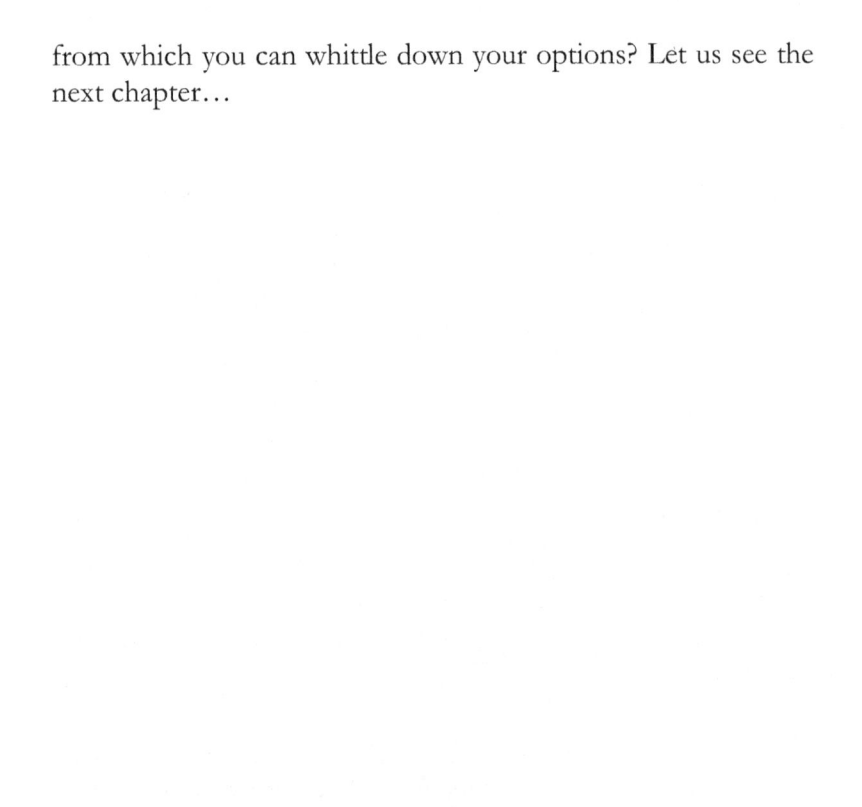

4

Consulting Your Advisors

Who in the world am I? Ah, that's the great puzzle! –Lewis Carroll

If you have ever read Lewis Carroll's greatest book for children, you would have come across this part in the second chapter, where a worried Alice is trying to introspect about who she really is. She tries to recall futilely everything she had learned and finally comes to the conclusion that she must have turned into her friend Mabel, who knew less than herself, Alice. She couldn't have known it, but perhaps Alice was undergoing her first-ever episode of *imposter syndrome*. Imposter syndrome is when you feel that you are not worthy of the success you achieve. It is characterized by crippling self-doubt and leaves you feeling like a fraud which has deceived people around you. When in the throes of imposter syndrome, people often feel that they will be unmasked shortly as the failures they really are. If you have ever felt this way, remember that you are not alone.

When Mariana Costa Checa completed her degree from the London School of Economics and Columbia University, she was stoked about starting a web development company in her native city of Lima, Peru. Her company did well, and she was pleased about its growth. But there was something that was nagging at her as well. She saw the abysmally small number of women who were coming forward to get employed, and she couldn't understand this. When she researched further into this problem, she realized that the tech field had been, by years of propaganda and a sort of tacit understanding, earmarked for men. Women were excluded simply because they were made to feel, at some stage, that it wasn't a field for them. She then

39

started Laboratoria, a unique school that encouraged women to get acquainted with technology so that the gender disparity in technological fields could be reduced. Laboratoria focused on women who were underemployed and underpaid and gave them relevant and current coding, designing, and other tech skills that would make them qualified to enter the job market in six months into highly competitive and high-paying roles. As per the latest statistics, over 2,400 women have come out of the portals of Laboratoria with an employment rate of over 85%! Mariana's company now has five training centers in countries like Mexico, Peru, Chile, and Brazil. She was recognized for her efforts by Barack Obama and Mark Zuckerberg. Mattel chose her as one of the women leaders on whom their latest model Barbie dolls were designed for the International Women's Day of 2019 (*Mariana Costa Checa, Co-Founder and CEO at Laboratoria*, 2022).

An elephant, which has been tied to a tree with a flimsy rope since its childhood, does not realize its strength to set itself free even when it grows into an adult. Many times, we are stuck with choices or options simply because of stereotypes and mental conditioning that tell us we can't do something or that we won't be good enough. Much like the intelligent and talented women that Mariana met, who believed that they weren't *smart enough* or *skilled enough* to enter the tech field, which had been a man's domain till then, we underplay our strengths, talents, and abilities.

This chapter should help you take a good stock of your potential, which will be instrumental in identifying that dream job of yours. It will also help you understand how different areas of employment are segregated by clusters so that you can slowly start taking a few picks.

Career Clusters

Again, let me gently remind you that this book does not intend to offer a definitive guide to all the careers available. However, wouldn't it be great to at least have a grouping of careers by the similarity of subjects involved in each of them? The sixteen career clusters, as per the National Career Clusters Framework of the US Department of Education, help with exactly this problem. Let's get cracking then, shall we?

- Agriculture, Food, and Natural Resources: This cluster includes every job that deals with agriculture, animal husbandry, food manufacturing or processing, or natural resources. Based on the specific area you choose, you could be a farmer, veterinarian, scientist, or even an engineer. One common factor that would bind you to others working in this area would be your love for the outdoors. Some of these roles require the completion of a specific degree, whereas others will require on-the-job training.

- Architecture and Construction: Do you love buildings and systems that hold a home or commercial structure together? Based on your aptitude, you could be an architect, engineer, carpenter, plumber, or mason. You may love working with, designing, or improving spaces. Again, some of these are more technical areas that require a formal degree. For all construction-related jobs, a love for math would be mandatory.

- Arts, Audio, Visual Technology, and Communications: Are you a creative person who loves to paint, write, or perform? Then this may just be the cluster you seek. Publishing, journalism, film, and theater are all professions that would fall under this. Some of these roles, like that of an actor, require only skill and talent, while others, like becoming a sound technician, will require the completion of a particular course. People who have a love for art, fashion, and aesthetics will most likely end up here.

- Business, Management, and Administration: Do you like working with numbers and people? Are you fired up just imagining managing a business or specific functions of a business-like HR or accounts? Then there are the kinds of jobs that you should be looking at. Everyone from a secretary to a certified public accountant would be united in their love for working from an office and would have strong communication skills allied with sharp business acumen.

- Education and Training: If your forte is teaching, working with students of a particular age group, or handling the administrative tasks associated with an educational institution, then this is where you fit. For these jobs, it is essential that you have a strong passion for imparting knowledge and possess the requisite degrees yourself. Along with strong communication skills and expertise in a particular subject, you will also demonstrate what it means to be an ideal role model.

- Finance: Some of these roles may overlap with the Business, Management, and Administration roles we discussed. Finance is for people who love math and want to work at money management and growth. Wealth management, accounting, and insurance are just some of the many professions that fall within this area. Again, clear communication and number-crunching abilities will hold you in good stead here.

- Hospitality and Tourism: If you love food, traveling, and enabling the best travel experiences for people, then look no further—this is the field you seek. A hotel manager, a flight attendant, and a chef have one thing in common—they love to serve their customers only the very best. Some of these professions will require going through grueling courses or training periods to get to the top level, while entry-level positions will require only a high school degree.

- Human Services: Do you love to work with people in specific areas? These may be things like being a make-up artist or counseling or therapy. Any and all types of counseling and personal grooming services will fall under this. Becoming a psychologist will require taking up a relevant bachelor's degree and then getting a license. Whereas becoming a hairdresser or manicurist will require, at the very least, a few years of apprenticeship.

- Information Technology: Do you like working with technology and incorporating internet solutions into your everyday life? You may plan to become a web developer, coding expert, computer science teacher, or network administrator. Well, as you may have guessed by now, these roles will require you to work long hours on the system in an office environment, though, for some roles, the flexibility of working remotely is also now available. Most of these roles will require you to stay updated because information technology evolves every single day.

- Law, Public Safety, Corrections, and Security: Do you have a strict sense of right and wrong? Do you often feel the need to implement fair and just practices in society that would benefit more people or reduce the marginalization of some sections of society? Law is now a vast area that includes things like criminal, consumer, and corporate law, as well as cybersecurity. So whether you want to become an attorney, police officer, or security guard, this is the cluster for you. Most of these specializations will require special degrees or training, and you will be working in a police station, courtroom, or office, depending on your profile.

- Manufacturing: These are jobs that require more of a direct physical engagement with the making of goods or products. Many of these jobs require only on-the-job training. However, there may be specific areas that require certification. You will be working in a busy factory if this is your preferred area. Machine operator, quality control of products, installation or repair of machines, etc., would be some roles that fall under this cluster. Trade degrees can sometimes assist you in obtaining such jobs.

- Marketing, Sales, and Service: Do you love to talk and persuade people to take a course of action? It looks like sales and marketing could be right up your alley. Of course, gone are the days when direct door-to-door selling was the only form of marketing. We have a wide array of marketing roles available today in print and visual media. If you have the words or the eye for what will sell, this could still be your area, even if you aren't the most outgoing person. As a marketing executive, your spoken or written communication must be excellent. Marketing overlaps with the IT segment because it, too, requires illustrators, animators, and designers. Most marketing roles look for talent rather than degrees, though a marketing degree can be beneficial. Depending on your role and the company you work for, you will work from home or an office.

- Science, Technology, Engineering, and Mathematics: STEM subjects will also overlap with IT but deal much more with core sciences and math. Most of these jobs

44

will require the completion of specific degrees, sometimes all the way up to a research degree. This is the space for scientists, biologists, and statisticians, among others. You have to have a deep love for your subject and a passion for keeping learning.

- Government and Public Administrations: The government has a variety of offices, including defense systems, revenue offices, public administrations, and so on. At the highest level, we know this translates as being a president, prime minister, or member of the police, but there are also more local roles available to work with your civic and city council authorities. There are specific degrees and licenses that you will have to qualify for should you ever feel pulled into a career in this line.

- Health Science: When I say, "Health Science," your first thought will be medicine or nursing. However, health today includes a lot of allied areas such as biomedical and biotechnological research, pharmaceutical and paramedical professions, and even emergency medical technologies. Most of these professions will involve working at a hospital, private clinic, patients' homes, or labs. They require very specialized degrees with relevant training. If you take up a job in this area, empathy and communication will be two vital skills to possess.

- Transportation, distribution, and logistics: If you are now mentally picturing driving a large truck filled with goods from a warehouse to a shop, you are only thinking of a part of what this profile includes. This cluster encompasses all jobs associated with transportation, supply, and delivery, including jobs like those of a parking attendant or a pilot. To be a pilot or driver, you need a license, while other related jobs might require training periods. People in this field have a passion for punctuality and logistics management.

Now that you may have a better understanding of where you stand, let us look at people who can help you with concrete choices and decisions that you may have to make in the near future.

Building Conversations on Career Choices—What? Why? Who?

First things first. Assume you have identified a potential career path. Why would you want ideas, opinions, and thoughts on it before you freeze on it? You must have heard the aphorism that "*two heads are better than one.*"

When you ask somebody who knows you well for their viewpoint, you are looking at a couple of questions to be answered:

1. Based on their knowledge of you and the subjects, do they think you will be a good fit for the role?

2. Based on your activities and extracurricular interests, what do they think of this job prospect for you?

3. Do they think that this career would be worth the investment you would be making in terms of time, effort, and money?

4. How do they view this profession in terms of a steady income for you?

5. Do they know of somebody in this profession personally, and could they put you in touch with them?

6. Do they think that this job would satisfy you in the long run?

These are just some of the questions you want to be answered. Yes, we all know that personal happiness is ultimately yours to find and choose. However, sometimes our perception of ourselves can be a little skewed. Talking to these people, who know you well, will give you a fresh perspective on how they see you. This might help you streamline your ideas and decisions further.

So who are these people you should definitely consult before making up your mind?

- Parents

- Teachers

- Guidance Counselors

- Coaches

I have listed the above in descending order of how well each of these categories of people will know you. Parents and teachers see you every day and might have witnessed some of your ups and downs, transformations, and mood swings. As such, they are people who would be very reliable for discussing your plans through and through.

Guidance counselors, if they are associated with your school, may know you to an extent if you have interacted with them consistently over the years. However, they will use your marks and performance in key areas to determine if what you have chosen will suit your temperament and overall nature. But you also have to remember that people who have never had any academic performance indicators have done extremely well in related areas. We know how several famous entrepreneurs never even completed a formal school degree. Guidance counselors will be able to give you a good indication of your expertise based on tangible reports, but they can only do so much in ascertaining the strength of your passion.

Career coaches are experienced and trained individuals who can generally spot specific talents in people. However, they too rely on the results of tests or other tangible indicators before they give you a concrete *nay* or *aye*. There is no harm in talking to these people but always listen to your inner voice as well while holding these conversations. You can ask them as many questions and clarifications as you may like and remember they do have a vast understanding of various professions and what it takes to succeed in them. However, as far as their assessment of your skills and talents goes, it need not be the final word.

Conversations on Careers Continued

Finally, let me quickly list some other spaces where you can listen in on experts talking about specific job opportunities.

- Career fairs: Have you been to book or art exhibitions or farmers' markets? Now imagine instead of the books, paintings, or farm products being sold, companies put up their booths to acquaint prospective talent with jobs that are available. That, in a nutshell, is a career fair for you. So what's your part here?

- You can carry your resume or latest CV with all your experience and achievements.

- Go armed with a list of questions you'd like to ask your employer.

- Get leads to people who are working in the area of your interest, whom you can contact later on.

- Interact with peers who may be searching for similar roles to get more ideas on courses, certifications, or experiences that will contribute to your resume.

- Job Communities: Schools and colleges offer you the chance to become part of a job community. This community will include people from the institution looking at similar career options or lines of work in the same area. Some of these may have access to mentors who will help you with general aspects of a job hunt, like crafting a resume and guiding you with interview skills, as well as more specific aspects of a particular area, like cracking a written round of assessment, etc.

What can you do as part of a job community?

- Ask lots of questions.

- Keep your eyes and ears open for opportunities, internships, and other related experiences.

- Participate in a one-on-one session or webinar with a mentor who can give you the inside scoop on the place you want to work.

- Search for opportunities to upskill yourself.

Is your head reeling with all this information? It's okay to take a moment to process it all. I know it can seem unnerving to have so many different avenues thrown at you. Take a breath; we have a long way to go, but you can choose to do this at your pace, and the further you go, the easier it will get, I assure you.

Key Points

Let's quickly recap how your scrutiny of yourself and conversations on careers can be better planned if you:

- Have an understanding of the sixteen career clusters and weed out those that aren't in keeping with your tastes, interests, or personality.

- Take the help of adults who know you and your potential and have experiences in the relevant field, like parents, teachers, career counselors, and coaches.

- Participate in career fairs or become active members of job communities.

How do you build a strong foundation for yourself? How can what you learn in the classroom complement what you learn outside of it? Let us march onward and learn...

5

Training

The most important thing we learn at school is the fact that the most important things can't be learned at school. –Haruki Murakami

The first time I read this quote, I laughed until I had tears in my eyes. The next time I came across it, it seemed so true that it didn't seem so funny anymore. Its true school has many pros and cons and can never be a substitute for real-life experience and some things that you pick up outside its walls. But if you asked me whether I think that school can be done away with, my answer would still be a resounding "no." It is true that schooling cannot provide you with all the answers to how you should live your life, but it can be the framework upon which you build your learning. In other words, if you limit your learning only to what is taught in school, you will end up like the proverbial frog in the well, who is content with tidbits in the well and thinks that it has experienced all the wonders that the world has to offer.

I am reminded of the well-known parable of the blind men who describe the elephant here. The first man who touches its trunk describes it as "a big, thick snake." The man who gets hold of the ears says the elephant is shaped like "a big fan." The one who touches its legs says the beast is like "a tree trunk," while a fourth man, holding its tail, says it is like "a rope." The fifth and sixth men, touching the side and the tusk of the elephant, say that it is like "a wall" and "a spear," respectively. What can we say? The elephant is like everything the men say and much more when put together! Your education, likewise, could be made up of the bits and pieces of what you gather at school and outside it and how you choose to place all this knowledge together.

The Tiers of the Education System

But first, what is the schooling system we are talking about?

Schooling systems throughout the world vary in the curriculum and subjects they offer. However, most countries adopt a tiered system of imparting education. For instance, schools in the US have three main tiers for schooling up to the twelfth standard.

- Elementary school: This school covers KG to standard five. Generally, students are placed in one classroom for a year, and one teacher handles the basics of English, Maths, Science, Social Studies, Physical Education, and Fine Arts.

- Middle school: Includes grades six to eight. Starting from this, students have teachers for each subject and are expected to shift classrooms and manage their time as they sit through each of their courses. Math, Science, English, and Social Studies continue to be core subjects, with electives like a foreign language, a vocational subject, business, writing, and so on. Depending on the school, you can choose a certain number of these electives based on your interests.

- High school: Includes classes nine to twelve. The lower high school comprises grades nine and ten; late high school comprises the eleventh and twelfth grades. Students continue with the same subjects as they learned in middle school, with more specialized electives. High school is intended to prepare students for the undergraduate or degree courses that they will encounter in college.

Call it by whatever name you will; different levels of schooling offer you the bones and muscles that make up the anatomy of your learning.

Have you ever put together a jigsaw puzzle? The individual pieces hardly seem to make any sense, but put them together, and voilà, you have just created the big picture. There is only one point of difference between a jigsaw puzzle and learning, though. The ultimate task of a jigsaw puzzle is for you to put together the final picture, and there is only one final picture possible.

Unless you are my niece, that is, and I'll tell you why a little later.

School is probably similar in that there is only one ultimate goal with schooling—obtaining the certificate and passing with a score that doesn't make you cringe every time you have to say it aloud.

However, there is no end to learning. There are an infinite number of ways in which what you learn can be arranged to provide you with material for new ideas. Now would be a good time to tell you why I think my three-year-old niece is a genius.

The following is a picture of the jigsaw puzzle I recently gifted her:

The following is what she created from it:

(Apologies for the blurriness; she was too excited with her creation to let me take a good photo.)

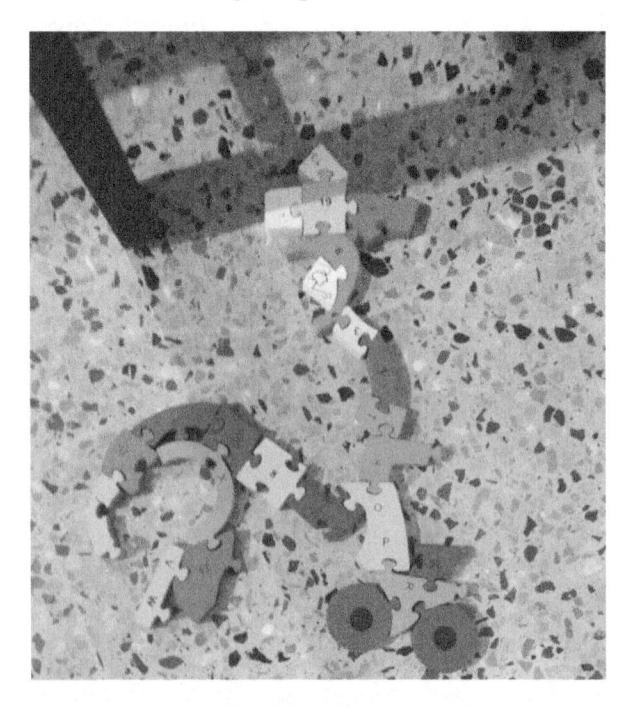

To reiterate, if you can make a moped out of a car puzzle, like my niece, you're probably on the right track!

When Do I Start Thinking of a Career?

From my experience, elementary school is too young for any child to be grappling with thoughts of a career or choice of profession. At this stage, I would encourage students to learn as much as possible and to have fun experimenting with subjects and ideas, meeting and interacting with friends and new people.

Middle school is generally considered a good time to start toying with the idea of what career you should choose. In fact, most research agrees that students at the middle school level are capable of identifying subjects and areas that interest them and that this is one of the best times to start talking with people and exploring more about hobbies, interests, and possible professional decisions (Cook & National Journal, 2014).

High school (grades nine and ten) and senior high school (grades eleven and twelve) are when you need to have a more concrete idea of where you want to be. I will be focusing on these two stages and looking at things you can do to get some idea of what you can do. So how can the choices you make in high school determine your future course? Let's see.

Early High School: The Freshman and Sophomore

The early high school years are ideal for establishing a career path. What are the concrete things that you can do that will help you move forward?

Let us look at this in a stepwise manner.

1. Talk: Some of your teachers may already be talking to you about possible careers and what you have to do to reach them. Talk to them individually about your love and what they feel about your potential towards them. They may also put you in touch with career counselors, program heads, or people in relevant and related areas whom you can talk to. Your parents are the other set of people who have to be constantly in the loop about your planning—not just because they know you and will be vital when you make those financial decisions, but also because they generally want only the best for you and your happiness.

2. Draw a career plan: Based on the subjects you choose, select at least three different career plans that are related but also different. One would be your ideal, and the other two would be backup options. For instance, a teacher of a language can also look at jobs in writing and editing. Remember, these are not final plans; you are just giving voice to the ideas in your head.

3. School grades: Yes, it can be a stressful time trying to manage your academics and other related assignments and projects, along with trying to chalk out a career plan. Fear not. Take up one course or activity that is a stress buster for you. Find time to enjoy the two beginning years of high school because, hey, that's also why schooling still exists. You know the old saying: "All work and no play makes Jack and Jill dull kids." However, and I will say this again, try your best to keep up your grades. Consistency of effort will pave the way here.

Late High School: The Junior and Senior

Based on the subjects you have chosen in your last two years of school, the junior and senior high school years, you will find that you do have a lot on your hands. Also, remember that if you are planning on applying to college, good grades will be essential, not just to determine your entry into the particular course that you are seeking but also to get scholarships that will help you and your family financially.

You can check online for the list of scholarships that your chosen college or institution provides its students and how you can become eligible for them. Students in the US can submit the Free Application for Federal Student Aid (FAFSA) so that the government can assess their eligibility for student financial aid. This is a free process and requires only a few mandatory requirements for applicants. There will be similar scholarships offered by most countries across the globe to deserving students to fulfill their dreams of pursuing bachelor's, master's, and even doctoral programs. Be sure to check out the resources available on your government's website's student help pages on a regular basis so that you can keep track of new scholarships or grants that may have been recently introduced.

Finally, a few words of general advice. Keep yourself motivated and on top of classwork so that there is no mountain of work piling up towards the time of exams. Remember to participate in your classes and build a rapport with your peer group, who will be your first point of contact when it comes to clarifications or questions about your studies. Over and above all, do not neglect your physical and mental health because, without it, all your grades and your performance on tests would be a waste indeed.

Beyond High School

Assume you have completed high school. Now what? Let us quickly run through the types of further education that you can consider and what each of them would mean for you in terms of a career. For a point of reference, we will be looking at the US model of education, but every country will have equivalents of the following types of education: We will also look at the types of institutions from which you would be taking your further degrees or certifications. Since visual learning has been said to be more effective, I have tried to collate the information you will need into the table below.

Type of Degree/ Certification	Number of Years to Complete	Credits	Focus	Type of Institution
Associate degrees like AA/ AS/ AFA/ AAB/ AAS	2	60	Help students gain entry-level jobs, basic skills	Community college/ College/ University

Type of Degree/ Certification	Number of Years to Complete	Credits	Focus	Type of Institution
Professional certifications	Depends on the course and usually ≤ 2 years	Depends on course	Job training and gaining specific skills like architecture, business, journalism, law, library science, optometry, pharmacy, public policy, human medicine, professional engineering, podiatric medicine, scientific dentistry, K-12 education, and veterinary medicine	Community colleges/ College

Type of Degree/Certification	Number of Years to Complete	Credits	Focus	Type of Institution
Career and technical education, also called vocational education	Depends on the course and usually ≤ 2 years	Depends on course	Skilled professions like electricians, mechanics, pharmacy technicians, dental hygienists, nuclear technicians, machinists	Community college/Trade school/Technical school
Apprenticeship—working with a professional in the subject	Depends on the course and usually < 1 year	Depends on course	Part of professional certification or technical education	Community college/Trade school/Technical school

Type of Degree/ Certification	Number of Years to Complete	Credits	Focus	Type of Institution
Bachelor's degree like BA/ BS/ BFA/ BArch/ BEng/ BPhil	4	120	A well-rounded education consisting of major and minor courses	College/University

Since I have used terms like "college" and "community college," let me quickly run you through what each of these means.

Types of Institutions

- Colleges: Colleges are either privately or publicly funded institutions that typically offer four-year degree programs and other courses. These may be affiliated with a larger university or be standalone institutions. State-funded institutions will be cheaper and more affordable than private ones.

- Universities: Colleges are either privately or publicly funded institutions that typically offer four-year degree programs and other higher degrees like master's and doctoral programs. State-funded institutions will be cheaper than private ones.

- Community Colleges: These are state-funded universities that offer undergraduate courses like two-year associate programs. They are more affordable than colleges. Most students start their four-year bachelor's degree at community colleges, complete an associate degree, and then transfer to a college or university to save costs.

- Trade schools: These are specialized institutions that offer skill-based learning for vocational courses and mostly include apprenticeships as well. They offer courses that will enable students to move into the workforce quickly.

Remember to research the institution you choose well and the types of job opportunities and placements they offer. Ensure that the college or university you choose is an accredited one, which means that it is recognized by the government authority for higher education.

Key Points

- Middle school is the ideal time to start thinking about career options.

- Use your first two years of high school to explore all the choices available.

- In your last two years of high school, sketch a working plan and backup options for your further course of study.

- Post high school, select a program that would suit your taste, is financially viable, and is at an institution that is accredited.

The next chapter will expand on some of these ideas and provide you with more alternatives on your voyage ahead.

6

Charting Your Course(s)

School is a lot like toilet paper. You only miss it when it's gone. – Unknown

Thinking back on my high school years, I can only remember cribbing about the amount of work that was expected from us poor students. I remember all the homework, the classwork, the projects, the lab classes, the computer classes, the tuition, and the grades we had to maintain to go anywhere. (Not reaching anywhere was a threat we used to hear A LOT!). I'd dream of the day I'd be free of school. Life always seemed cooler outside of school. It seemed all of us couldn't wait for our careers and our futures to unfold, where we could earn, do things on our own steam, and not be told to do this or that. Well, you know what? We were sadly mistaken. Now when I think back on school, it was easy, with the toughest part being to just show up and be told what to do! We only had to do one thing—study and complete tests and assignments in our chosen subjects—and, with the exception of those who had made a poor choice and may have felt stuck in the wrong field, most of us knew, even back then, that these were areas that interested us.

Nobody told us then that adulting, which we were all dying to get into, was going to be so much more hectic and chaotic. We have work, families, taxes to pay, and kids to take care of, and just as you think you can at least be done thinking about school, subjects, and marks, you will find that your kids are going through the same anxieties that you went through not very long ago. You'd like to tell them that things are only going to get easier, but you know that this is probably not the truth. You know that school and high school are probably where they'll have it easiest and real life will bring bigger complications and a more erratic set of concerns as each seeps into the other. Believe me, when I say that high school can be a lot of fun, but only if you are a little more organized. You can learn a lot from here, even if it won't come close to the *real-life skills* that only life and experiences can give you.

You'll be thinking, and rightly so, *Why go through with high school if it doesn't give me anything?* Now hold your horses, mate. I never said anything about a school not providing you with anything. All I'm saying is that school is much easier than real life. And yes, one of the things that school will equip you with is to own your sh*t! That's right. Like everything else in life, school is a field where you will have multiple things thrown at you (on a miniature scale), and how you learn to handle these things will define how well you handle your life as well.

Think of driving, if you will. Some of you here must have definitely attended the simulated driving lessons—a version of Road Rash or Forza Horizon 5 that actually teaches you to drive. Now, a simulated driving class may not beat the experience of taking your car or bike out on a busy street and learning to maneuver yourself through it, but it is better than nothing. Even the simulated class will give you a lot of ideas about what you should be watching out for, how quickly your reflexes should kick in, and possible mistakes you may make when you are trying to keep track of what is in front of you, behind you, and on both sides of you. So yes, high school is not real life, but it is a start.

In 2010, Nimali Gunawardana only hoped to start a business that would give vent to her fiery ambition. She was 25 years old and had already worked as a sewing machine operator in a garment shop and even as a gardener prior to that. She had always dreamed of starting a business that would give back to the society of which she was a product, and also because her country had sponsored her education. Her first attempt to start the business ended in huge losses for her and for the lenders. So when she persevered and wanted to do the same a second time, her parents were against it. But she persisted and converted a mentorship opportunity with Youth Business Sri Lanka and a modest loan of $781 into a business of $39,000, equivalent to 5.1 million Sri Lankan rupees at the time in 2013. Needless to say, she was able to pay off all her debts and employed 13 people from the local community as well. Her factory, Nimali Chips, and Fibre Mill, focused on three main products: coir, coir pith, and husk chips used to manufacture rope grow material for plants and filter water. In 2013, Youth Business Sri Lanka named her the Start-up Entrepreneur of the Year (Smale, 2013).

As Nimali herself concedes, though she had a fire in her belly, what really helped her to succeed the second time was the mentorship that she received from Youth Business. Sometimes all it takes is a little direction for the fruition of your dreams!

So let's see some courses that you can take up and some positive attitudes that you can inculcate, maybe even before high school, that will help you do well in life, shall we?

Sorting Your Priorities

A lot of high school (and life) boils down to how well you can plan your time in terms of the things that have to be done. You have to reduce all the things to be done into lists of life-and-death priorities, top but not urgent priorities, and long-term priorities. Then, of course, there are the things that aren't priorities but have to be tackled eventually. So let us look at three important aspects of this: (1) classes to take to improve your chances at college; (2) essential courses that will aid future studies; (3) how to tackle studies.

Classes That Will Aid College

Let us quickly run through the subjects that colleges will look for most when they look at student applications and the combinations of classes that will help you be noticed.

- English: Whatever you do, you need to communicate well to tell people your objectives and how you hope to achieve them. Four years of English at the high school level will equip you with the writing, speaking, and reading skills that will give you an edge over others.

- Math: Many colleges look for mandatory three years of math at the high school for admission, whereas there are more competitive institutions and courses that will require you to have four years of math at the high school. Aptitude in algebra and geometry will always be rewarded, whatever STEM course you set your heart on. Take basic math early so that you can opt for advanced-level courses in the later years of high school. You could choose from viable combinations of Geometry, Trigonometry, Algebra I, Algebra II, Precalculus, and Calculus.

- Science: Most colleges will look for at least three years of lab classes in science. Your chances at college will be improved by taking at least one year each of biology, chemistry, physics, and earth or physical science. Advanced courses in these will give you an extra year of science, which may be required for admissions to more competitive colleges or courses.

- Social studies: It encompasses everything that has happened to people worldwide. You can take up courses in U.S. History and Governance, Geography, and Economics.

- Foreign Language: At least two years of expertise studying a foreign language will show colleges that you are a person willing to go beyond the necessities of the academic framework. Certain colleges may require you to complete four years of study in a foreign language too.

- Arts: At least a few colleges would like to see if you have an interest in things that have, through the centuries, made humans creative and give them their unique sense of vision. You can show your participation in courses like Drama, Art, or Music to better recommend yourself to them better.

Though these would perhaps constitute a minimum requirement for your application to higher education, we shall also go one step further and look at some advanced or challenging courses that you can also explore while still in high school.

Higher Level Courses

If you are comfortable with the regular syllabus covered in class and want to taste what college-level courses will feel like, there are a few options available to you right in your high school. These are mostly the same subjects that you will be doing, but more in-depth than the regular classes. Yes, they will require more work, but they will also help you get placed in a better college of your choice and probably make your higher education path easier.

The following are some options you have when it comes to higher-level courses:

- Honors Classes: These are more or less the same subjects that you will deal with in high school, but these classes will be paced faster and will cover the subject in a more thorough or in-depth manner. Clearing these exams will show the potential colleges you apply to that you may be ahead of your peers in terms of subject knowledge.

- Advanced Placement (AP) Program: This is a course offered by the College Board in some countries. University-level courses and examinations are on offer to college students who feel they can tackle them. Good grades in these exams will mean that the student will get placements in good colleges and equivalent course credits. There are currently thirty-eight courses available under this program.

- International Baccalaureate (IB) Program: IB is an internationally recognized board and syllabus. Students taking courses affiliated with the IB get an IB high school diploma. There are about six groups of subjects like Language and Literature; Language Acquisition; Individuals and Societies; Sciences; Mathematics; and the Arts. Each of the first five courses is mandatory, plus either one more from the sixth or one more from the five groups.

- College Courses: If your school has a dual enrollment facility, you may be able to take college-level courses either at school or at a nearby college campus. If you clear exams in these courses, it will earn you course credits and look good on your college application.

Now that we know what classes and courses can make an impression when it comes to enrolling in higher education. Let us also look at how methods of study can help you understand the subject better and improve your grades as well.

How Do I Study?

Studies (akin to prayers, I would venture) are ultimately very personal things. Everyone has methods that work for them and don't. For instance, we are told ever so often about the peer group study model. I was told more than once that if you team up with your friend and study, it will be beneficial for both of us. But it never did for me. Whenever I met up with a friend to study, everything other than actual studies would happen. We would gossip, snack, watch TV, and play video games, and by the time we'd have to part, we'd realize we had not even touched the book. On the rare occasions when I'd discipline myself to take the book out when with my friend, I'd find their pace too slow or too fast for me. But there was something that did work. Somewhere during high school and my early college days, I discovered I was a good explainer. When a friend wanted me to explain a portion to them, I could do that with ease. I would prepare on my own and then convey what I learned to them the next morning. I could see that it was doing wonders for my understanding of the subject and my retention powers. Moreover, it improved my ability to communicate my understanding of the subject to them.

So, though you have to find out what makes you tick, here are some general tips when it comes to acing those tests.

- The longest way around is the shortest way home: You know what's harder than studying? Having so many things to do that you don't know where to begin. So start by making a schedule and always giving more priority to things that are harder. Yes, you heard me. If you are sweating over algebra but not so much over English, then perhaps you need to allot more time to algebra and less to English.

- Do not bite off more than you can chew: No, I'm not talking about snack breaks here. Set for yourself small, doable chunks of time at a time so that you don't have one look at your to-do list and go, "I'm never going to complete this anyway," and close your books. When you complete a smaller section, you will naturally feel inclined to do more. Start early and do smaller sections over longer spells of time rather than trying to cover a huge part of the syllabus in a short span.

- Old habits die hard: Are you a person who loves a good nap? Then stop studying on your bed; it will only tempt you to fall asleep. Do you love the internet as a distraction? Keep the phone away. But keep a bottle of water and a few (healthy) snacks at your disposal so that you don't have to waste time searching for them when you start feeling peckish. The more you stick to a schedule, the easier it will be to stick to it in the long run.

- Practice makes perfect: Test your learning. Take online mock tests or have your teacher give you summaries or questions based on the sections that you cover. Let your friends ask you questions about the topics that you've decided to cover. Choose a study guide or textbook that contains both simple and difficult problems that you can work out. Try out more application questions on a theory you might have just learned. And finally, check the answers. Do not be disheartened if you get them wrong. But do find out what mistake you made. These are just some ways to test your understanding.

The above are some things that helped me with my studies, and I hope they'll come in handy for you (please note the trouble I went to over selecting the right proverb for each of those tips). In the next section, we will look at some tests that may help you stay ahead of your peers and may help you with the college applications that you will make shortly.

Testing Waters

There is an old English proverb that goes, "Weighing a pig doesn't fatten it." It is true. You don't become better at something by taking a series of tests without pausing to learn the content or understand the subject thoroughly. I am not asking you to take unnecessary tests when you aren't sure of your caliber. However, with proper preparation, there are a couple of tests that you could consider, which may shorten your odds of gaining a seat in the college that is closest to your heart or of doing a course abroad, and so on.

- Preliminary Scholastic Aptitude Test and Scholastic Aptitude Test (PSAT and SAT): The College Board administers these tests, which give a lot of weight to math, verbal ability, and reasoning skills. These will help you access college courses, scholarships, and state funding for your higher education. I will not bore you with a detailed schedule of the exam. But if you are interested, you can check the official website and start preparations.

- American College Testing (ACT): This is a standardized test provided by the ACT, Inc., for college intake. It provides an online examination to test the written, verbal, numerical, and scientific aptitude of students.

- The International English Language Testing System (IELTS) and the Test of English as a Foreign Language (TOEFL): These are both standardized and widely recognized tests in the English language catered to non-native speakers of English who wish to enroll in universities where English will be the medium of instruction. Both of these tests the candidate on the four components of the language, namely, reading, writing, listening, and speaking. When you apply to particular colleges or universities, check which of the two tests they prefer—IELTS or TOEFL.

We have covered how certain courses or advanced certifications will give you an edge over other candidates. In the following section, we will now see how you can go about selecting the best college depending on the subjects you prefer.

Searching for a College

A college, like a glove, should be the right fit for you and your budget. So how can we find the right place where you will be happy, and which will suit all your other needs? Here are some resources that will help you fine-tune your search and some general tips to help you prepare for your application.

Some Resources

Here I will enumerate a few resources that you can browse through to clear your queries on courses, classes, and the procedure to apply to colleges.

Online Resources

Since I am not writing a book only catering to students of a single country, I may not be able to give you lists of resources linking to options available in your country. However, I will provide a set of guidelines for whenever you use online resources.

- Reliability: Check whether the website is sponsored by the government, a well-known higher education agency, or a news or press service. The information you get from these pages will be reliable. There may be websites that list colleges based on insider information—student reviews and such. Take them with a pinch of salt because reviews can be biased too.

- Currency: Check the date. Say you seek admission to the 2024 course. The resources and websites you use must contain facts that are not older than 2017 and preferably post-2020 if possible. (Remember, the pandemic has impacted even education systems worldwide.)

- Relevance: The internet will contain huge volumes of information, not all of which might be relevant to you. Learn to sift through it for things that will really impact you. Hone your search words until you get what you are seeking.

- Accuracy: Some of the websites will list figures or statistics from older web pages. Thus, cross-verify your findings with multiple sources. This will give you a better representation of what's correct.

Books

I am sure there will be books that catalog colleges, their facilities, courses, fees, and other details that you seek. The following are best-selling college guides for education in the USA. If you can find comparable guides for your country, it would be great. When you select a book, be sure to read customer reviews for it on Amazon so you get a good idea of what aspects the book covers.

- *Fiske Guide to Colleges* (2023) by Edward B. Fiske.

- *The Complete Book of Colleges, 2021: The Mega-Guide to 1,349 Colleges and Universities* (2021) by The Princeton Review.

- *Colleges Worth Your Money: A Guide to What America's Top Schools Can Do for You* (2020) by Andrew Belasco, Dave Bergman, and Michael Trivette.

In the following and last section of this chapter, let us look at two important aspects related to college admissions—i.e., facing interviews and getting selected to the IVY league of schools.

Facing Interviews

Congrats! You may have cleared all the tests and requirements and gotten a call letter from your favorite institution. But there is one last hurdle to clear—the dreaded interview. Relax. Interviews are a lot less challenging if you are even a little prepared for them and have the right attitude.

Before getting to the questions, a word of advice: Be the best version of yourself. Be well-groomed, dress semi-formally if not formally, hold yourself confidently, but be pleasant (which means to smile and look people in the eyes when you talk to them). Take time to process the question before you speak, and never be in a hurry to start talking. Use a not-too-loud but audible and well-modulated voice. It is perfectly fine to use a mirror to practice answering before you attend the real interview.

The Questions

Remember that the questions your panel or interviewer will ask are based on your life, hobbies, and projects that you have undertaken. Be clear and precise, and do not ramble. However, do qualify your statements with more than a mere yes or no.

The following are some questions most students get asked frequently:

1. Why did you choose to apply to this college or university?

2. Why do you feel the course you have applied for will be a good fit for you?

3. What was the last book you read? Or, what are you reading now?

4. How would you describe yourself? Or, how would your friends describe you?

5. What would you describe as your greatest weakness?

6. Talk about your strengths. Or, one achievement of yours.

7. Think of a situation that was challenging for you and how you overcame it.

8. If selected, in what ways do you think you can contribute to the culture and achievements of the institution?

You can browse online, and frame answers for these using the tips given. But remember to make them unique and in line with your tastes, opinions, and ideas. The last thing you want is for the board to reject you as a counterfeit.

Preparing for Ivy League

Ivy League colleges are well-established, the best internationally rated, and the most prestigious schools in the US. Harvard, Princeton, Yale, Cornell, Dartmouth, and Columbia Universities are all members of the Ivy League. They have a very limited student admission rate, and to make the cut, you have to be exceptionally brilliant or hardworking, or a combination of both. We have covered a few of the things that are prerequisites for admission to these schools, like good academic performance and high SAT or ACT scores.

The three other things that you will have to work towards during your high school years are:

1. Personal essays and statements of purpose as to why you want to study at a particular institution for a course and how you see this experience shaping your career and future plans.

2. Letters of recommendation from teachers, guides, and other people who know you in a professional or academic capacity and who can vouch for your high caliber, determination, and skills.

3. A strong passion for any one extracurricular activity (such as sports, arts, hobbies, community service, business, science, or technology) with honors, awards, or recognition won in your chosen area.

Remember that some of these criteria will vary from one institution to the next but that most of these colleges are looking for changemakers and trailblazers.

Key Points

- Learn to prioritize subjects and courses, which will help you with college admissions.

- Set aside dedicated hours, a place, and habits of study to ace your exams.

- Search for colleges and courses that would suit you academically and temperamentally.

- Be yourself while facing those stiff college interviews.

- The Ivy League is not a piece of cake, but with smart, hard work, you can make it.

Let us move forward and take a look at what you need to get a job and be successful at it.

7

Diving into Combat

Don't confuse having a career with having a life. –Hillary Clinton.

Sophia Amoruso was 22 years old, had worked *sh*t jobs* (her words), and was then stuck in a dead-end job at the security desk of an art school in 2006 when she thought she'd open an eBay store for secondhand clothes. She collected vintage clothes from thrift shops, used her friends as models, styled those pieces on them, took photos, marketed, and sold the attire online. Very soon, she found that her venture was a grand success. She named her store Nasty Girl, after the title of an album by singer Bette Davis. The followers were so many that Nasty Girl had to open a website of its own and earn its first-ever capital of $50 million from venture capitalists. Though uninitiated in business, Sophia was hardworking and relentless. She capitalized on ideas that worked and discarded those that didn't. She captured the essence of her business model in her 2014 book, *#GIRLBOSS*. Eventually, Sophia stepped down as CEO, and Nasty Girl was acquired by the BooHoo Group. Today Sophia Amoruso runs Girlboss Media, a company that creates videos and podcasts for women and organizes Girlboss Rallies, mentorship classes, and events for women (*About Sophia Amoruso*, 2020). What worked for Sophia was her ability to keep searching for a career that she was passionate about and that worked for her. Nasty Girl and Girlboss have both been attempts by Sophia to make the most of untapped potential in the world.

When you hunt for a job, one of the first requisites of the jobs that you apply for should be that they should keep you happy, not just now when you begin your career but also in the long run. Thus, it has to be related to a product, service, or ethic that you are truly excited about and passionate about. Let us now move on to the crux of job hunting.

Job Hunting and Preparation

In the earlier part of their careers, most youngsters are so desperate to make money that they'd be willing to take on anything that would pay their food, rent, monthly installments, and other obligations. Nobody really pauses to reflect on things like job satisfaction or personal growth. This is okay. Maybe initially, you can while away some time by just getting and settling into a job—any work culture will do. But this will not sustain you. Just any and every job will not lead to happiness. So what must you do?

Doing What Is Right vs. What Makes You Happy

I hark back to the very first story I mentioned in this book, the one about my friend. She had so many choices thrown at her. People kept rooting for her to become a doctor or an engineer. But just taking a course in the sciences was enough to tell her that's not where her heart lay. Chartered accounting, though chosen by herself, could kindle but not hold her attention. What she really loved was reading, writing, and creating. When she found her real interest, she could do a lot more than she ever intended because it was interesting, and she thrived off the excitement that it could provide her. The moral? Your career, like your future spouse, should pique and sustain your interest. Life is too short to hang onto somebody else's expectations.

As I have mentioned before, self-assessment of what you love and where you see yourself is a valuable skill here. I would like to reiterate one disclaimer here. Even though a lot of job sites will ask you to take personality and career tests to find a job that suits you, I would advise you to be very careful. An online test is too generic to give individualized or person-specific results. Though you can use these to perhaps find a general direction, I would suggest you talk to friends, parents, teachers, and career counselors before making the ultimate decision.

Where Do I Start?

Earlier, the primary source of finding jobs was the newspapers; today, it is no longer so. There are a variety of professional and job portals that will help you find the right job. I have already said it, but create profiles for yourself on well-known professional networking sites such as Indeed, LinkedIn, Glassdoor, Monster (now called Foundit), Craigslist, or CareerBuilder. Between these portals, you are sure to find plenty of jobs to apply for, and if you are lucky, employers might even contact you. Apart from this, most of these platforms help you boost employability skills, such as crafting a good resume, enhancing your communication skills, and much more.

Understanding the Industry

It is essential to really understand how your industry works and what the pros and cons are. For instance, there are sectors like real estate that go through boom-and-bust periods. You have to be prepared with alternative professional choices in periods when the industry could be going through a waning phase. This is true of traditional job markets as well. Whenever there is an economic recession, there could be layoffs that would affect many types of work profiles. Thus, one of the first things that you have to research is the present and future value of your job. In other words, how lucrative and sustainable the job is right now and what opportunities it will give me eventually, say, five or ten years down the line.

Expectations vs. Reality

Always be prepared for surprises. Your expectations from a job may not match what really happens. Even a field you think is inspiring could turn out to be much more repetitive and routine when you actually get into it. This is why I suggested talking to experts, job shadowing, and doing internships or apprenticeships in one of the earlier chapters. Your expectations will be more realistic if you know what really happens behind the scenes.

Understanding the Requirements to Get Selected

When you apply for a job, identify a list of things they require from applicants to qualify. This will help you stay more organized when you actually submit your application.

This includes, but is not limited to, the following:

- Proof of education, like marks or grade transcripts.

- Academic or professional references or contacts who can vouch for you. Do remember that many good companies no longer ask for recommendation letters but may still require you to provide details of your reporting manager or HR from your previous employment.

- Biodata or a resume should include all your experiences relevant to the role.

- Group discussion or interview.

In the next section, we will look at ways to strengthen your resume and how to present yourself in the best light when giving an interview.

Resume

Your resume is a manuscript to market yourself. It must never exceed two pages in length (employers hardly ever have the patience to read all of it) or include irrelevant details in it (a sure way of having it cast into the dustbin). However, it should provide your educational and professional experiences along with all the relevant skills you possess that you think would qualify you for the job. Put all the relevant information in bullet points that aren't repetitive or boring to look at.

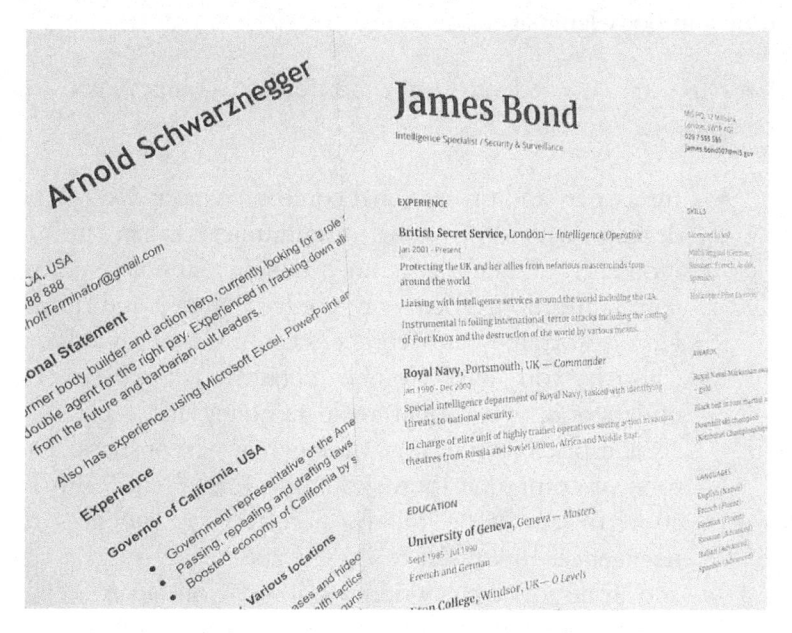

Above are interesting samples of resumes that I found online. Forget for a moment its fictional nature, but do you see how a lot of thought has gone into the wording and structuring of the document to make it readable, contain all relevant details, and yet be concise? There are no right or wrong ways to craft a resume. But how it looks to the reader could decide whether you are shortlisted for the next stage or not.

The Whole Gamut of Communication Skills

Communication matters. Not just in hunting for and holding down a job but even in your interpersonal relationships with friends and family. And unlike what you might be thinking right now, communication is not just about speaking! It includes the way you hold yourself, how expressive you are, your body language, and even your expressions. In fact, the words we utter account for a very small percentage of the actual communication that happens. The rest of it is determined by tone and body language.

Let us try to identify the different components of communication:

- Interviews and professional communication: We will be dealing with non-verbal communication in just a moment. When we are talking about spoken communication, focus on content, tone, and pitch. How you frame your sentences can say a lot about you. Though you have to be detailed enough to be understood, you should avoid rambling and repetition. A high pitch is indicative of anger or nervousness. The tone of communication should be formal and calm. A short or curt tone will be perceived as rudeness or negligence. In written communication, too, the content and tone of your writing will set you apart. Your communication should always be clear, concise, and polite (as opposed to clear but brusque or unfriendly).

- Grooming: Grooming is not just about maintaining personal hygiene. (Though please do be attentive to things like hair, facial hair, and oral or body odor because when you are hemmed in with your colleagues in the confines of an office for eight hours or more, not maintaining basic cleanliness constitutes a personal crime in my dictionary.) It is also about finding a style that is professional and yet uniquely yours. Confidence stems from the fact that you love your appearance, too. So figure out ways of dressing that will enhance your personality and personal style and are in keeping with company policies. Many companies are very liberal when it comes to ethnic hairdos and styles. You don't always need to compromise your identity to fit in.

- Body language: It determines how reliable and confident a person appears. Remember when your mother would pick on you not to slouch and to walk with your shoulders thrown back? She had a point. If you do not exude confidence, nobody will want to hire you. There are four components to non-verbal communication: expressions, posture, gestures, and eye contact. Always adopt an open, friendly, and relaxed expression so that people will know you are approachable. But also draw your limits; you want to be approachable, not a doormat on whom people will walk over. One last thing I would like to emphasize here is the distance you maintain while speaking to others. When talking to people, you may have to maintain a certain physical proximity to be audible, but never encroach on another's physical space. It is not just rude; it will be deemed an invasion of privacy. There are many more nuances to body language that you can research online and in books.

- Giving and receiving respect: Respect has to be earned. It is not something you can demand from others. A good part of the respect you earn will be dependent on the respect you give others. Respect is not about the unquestioning agreement in all matters, either. You can disagree with ideas. But always remember to keep conversations non-confrontational and constructive. The focus should always be on what can be done rather than on blaming somebody. Being kind and polite can be powerful weapons, even in your professional space. But ensure that nobody treats it as a weakness and tries to take advantage of your empathy for people.

- Professionalism: You can be friendly and yet professional. This would include things like being punctual, responding to mail or reminders in a timely manner, and maintaining responsibility, decorum, accountability, and excellence within the office. In other words, you always strive to do your best as far as possible, taking on responsibility and being personally accountable for your share of the work. Your ethics and integrity are also part of your professional attributes.

- Soft skills: Communication, problem-solving, creativity, and your emotional quotient, all taken together, will be important in landing and holding any job that you take up. Soft skills will also play a big role in providing solutions for emerging employee-friendly measures, such as encouraging diversity in hiring, raising employee mental health awareness, taking action against workplace harassment, and providing work flexibility. The right blend of technical and soft skills is something that employers will always be looking for.

There are just two other topics with which I'd wind up this chapter, which I think are very important, no matter the kind of job you take up.

Negotiating Employer and Employee Expectations

It is always best to have a clear understanding of employer expectations before you commit yourself to a job. Even at the interview stage, there are a few questions you can ask the prospective employer to understand what exactly it would take to succeed in your role.

You can think of questions like:

1. What would the day-to-day responsibilities of this job involve?

2. How would you describe the work culture of the organization?

3. Would this role involve overtime and travel on a regular basis?

4. Would I be part of a team or an individual contributor?

5. To whom would I be reporting?

These are just a few questions I would ask my hiring manager. Asking pertinent questions also shows that you are interested in building a career as opposed to merely getting a job for money's sake. It would demonstrate your willingness to integrate yourself into the work culture of the organization and will put you in a favorable light during the hiring process.

There is also the other side of the bargain. You should have an equally clear understanding of what you can expect in terms of personal and professional growth. Professional growth would include things such as increments, hikes, and promotions and the measurement criteria for them. Personal growth would comprise aspects such as what you can learn from the role and the concrete skills you would be acquiring, and how this would help you in the years to come.

Some questions you can ask yourself and find out more about with regard to employee expectations are:

1. Where do I see myself 2–5 years later in this sector?
2. Will I get mentorship to improve my skills and knowledge?
3. What is the likelihood of getting promotions based on my performance?
4. How much job security would I have in this job?
5. What are the other job perks?
6. Will I have a work-life balance in this role?

When you give an interview, it is important to understand both sides of the story before making a decision.

The Ladder of Success

It is easy to overestimate your prowess and skills. But always remember how competitive the job market is. Every employee feels they are entitled to certain perks and privileges, and sometimes it is just impossible for your employer to accommodate every such demand, even if they are generally fair in their treatment of employees. Also, remember that there are no shortcuts to success and that perseverance does eventually pay. Contrary to popular belief, there is no shame in working your way up to better jobs and higher pay. It will also perhaps give you a better understanding of the operations of your company.

It is important to have a clear picture of how promotions work, whether there are fair and transparent mechanisms in place to facilitate them, and how employee contributions are measured. You can also check whether your company hires internally for other departmental openings and what that would mean in terms of a salary hike. Sometimes, all you have to do is make the right move at the right time within the same organization, and it will make a world of difference for your designation and salary. Most people who are happy in their fields switch companies every 3–5 years, which is also a great way of getting industry-standard raises. Ultimately, you have to keep your eyes and ears open to find what moves and switches would be best for you to grow in your field. The importance of professional networking cannot be emphasized enough here.

Key Points

- To be successful at your job, you need to weigh the pros and cons of personal satisfaction vs. entering an established field just because you are qualified or because people expect you to do so.

- Job hunting could be a long-drawn-out affair. So sift through all your options. Make use of online job portals. Craft a resume that captures your voice accurately, and works on your communication. Get insider views on the field, company, and role you have in mind.

- Always ask questions to get a fair idea of the employer–employee expectations from a job.

- There is no shame in working your way up. It is insanely gratifying to go up the ladder of success. You can improve your chances of getting the perks of working for your organization or an industry by cultivating a clique of like-minded people and studying the switches and moves they make.

Next, have you thought of becoming an entrepreneur or being self-employed? Maybe it's not as hard as you think!

8

Becoming a Freelancer

Being your own boss is great. You get to choose which 18 hours a day you work. –Unknown

Did you know that the word "freelancer" actually comes from two words that literally mean "independent soldier?" In Sir Walter Scott's *Ivanhoe* (1819), he coined the term to stand for a knight whose lance was not pledged to the service of any one lord. A "freelancer" fought for money or for a personal cause. In the early 20th century, the Oxford Dictionary changed this word to its modern form.

Let me break up my style a bit here and start this section with a fable titled *The Three Little Fish* instead of a true-life story. The fable goes as follows:

Once upon a time, there were three fish who were fast friends. The first little fish was a bit lazy. It always lived in the past, thinking of the good times it had and never caring much about the future. The second fish was smarter. It lived in the present and was a good decision-maker. Though not a planner, it knew to come up with ideas as the situation demanded. The third friend, however, was the smartest of them all. It thought ahead and was always planning things for the future. Despite their different attitudes to life, the three of them got along well and spent their days happily playing games on the riverbed.

One day, two fishermen came to the river and were heard talking to each other. One of them said to the other, "Let's fish here. I hear the catch here is very promising. Mr. Santal says that all the fishes here are fat and juicy." The second man replied, "Yes. That's a good plan. However, I feel we haven't brought the right fishing gear today. Let's come back here tomorrow with the big nets. For today, we'll just go to our usual spot." The first man agreed, and they moved off.

The three little fish who had been listening in on the whole conversation began discussing what to do. The first fish said, "I think they won't come back. Let's just forget it and go and play, please." The second fish said, "They said they'd come back only tomorrow. Come, let's go. We'll see what to do tomorrow." The third fish, who was the wisest among them, said, "But didn't you hear? They are definitely coming back to catch us. I know of a canal that leads to a pond on the other side, by the banyan tree. Let's go there, and then we'll decide what to play."

But the first two fish were stubborn. The first one said, "What's all this fuss about nothing?" The other one added, "Fish and fiddlesticks! I'd like to see them catch me." The three friends quarreled that day. The third fish swam out into the pond, while the first two stayed back in their river.

The next morning, just as they had said, the two men came back with big nets. With the first haul, our two fish friends were caught. The second fish, who was clever and had a good head for making choices on the fly, came up with a plan. It played dead. The man who caught it took one look at the seemingly dead fish and said, "Yuck! Look at this dead one. It could be stale. I'm dropping it back." Saying this, he threw it back into the river. The smart little fish swam away to safety.

The first fish, our lazy little chap, had neither the foresight to save itself in advance nor the presence of mind to think up a plan now. It got trapped in the net, and as it was hauled up, writhing, and gasping for air, it died!

What's the message this story provides? In life, the people who get ahead are the ones who plan and prepare for the future. The next best to them are the ones who can deal with things as they come along and make firm decisions. If you can neither plan ahead nor deal with problems on the spot, then you too will flounder like our poor, first little fish (*A Panchatantra Story*, 2023).

Sometimes it makes a lot of sense to venture out on your own for things that you are certain of or passionate about. Without the gumption to move on your own, you could very well get stuck in a tight spot like the second little fish. If, after getting stuck, you don't have the resourcefulness to extricate yourself from the tight spot, it could very well spell the end of your career.

Why not consider ways to strike out on your own? Yes, we will be talking about self-employment: pros, cons, and ways in this chapter.

Self-Employment Meaning and Means

The Merriam–Webster dictionary defines self-employment as "the state of being self-employed," which is further defined as "earning income directly from one's own business, trade, or profession rather than as a specified salary or wages from an employer." Self-employment refers to running a business on your own or earning wages by selling products or services that you create or source from somewhere. In other words, there is no fixed salary, and you don't have an employer.

This sounds fun in theory, but in practice, like in any other job, it requires quite a bit of dedication and responsibility. Since there is no fixed income, you will have to account for lean periods when there may not be buyers or clients. If it still sounds exciting, what are we waiting for? Let's get started!

Considerations to be Self-Employed

Well, as it turns out, being self-employed takes some amount of investment, if not in money, then at least in a plan, your time, and energy. The following is a blueprint of how you could go about planning and implementing your self-employment plan.

- Make the decision, and take the plunge: This could be the hardest part. Especially if you have a full-time job now, it may be scary to turn to a path that is not as predictable as the job you have been at for ages. If it is a field that you want to try and if you have the time, you could give it a try even as you continue to hold on to your full-time job. Alternatively, depending on your financial commitments, you could set a timeframe and achievable targets for the business or freelance job you want to engage in. If you are able to achieve the targets in that time frame, you can perhaps think of the new venture on a more permanent basis.

- Identify your market: You will have to thoroughly research the target audience in terms of age, gender, ethnic backgrounds, etc., and decide to whom and how you are going to market your skill, product, or service. If you select too wide an audience, marketing will prove too cumbersome a task. If you select too narrow an audience, then you may not find enough customers, and your business may not prove feasible. The type of marketing you choose should be determined by the age bracket of your customer base. For instance, social media marketing is usually aimed at a younger age group, while TV or newspaper commercials would work better for an older generation.

- Increase your visibility: Any new business will take time to attract customers and grow a loyal base of customers. As part of marketing and building a brand image, you will have to use social media and ad campaigns to make yourself known. It will include the A-Z of getting clients, managing feedback, and reaching out to a wider pool of people.

- Administrative fundamentals: Depending on where, what, and how you go about selling, find out if you have to register your business or trade. You may also need specific licenses or permits to run the business, especially if you have a physical shop. You will have to get in touch with a financial expert or a government authority to shed more light on whether this is necessary and how to do it.

- Put in a system: When you start a business or venture, you have to put systems in place. What rates will you set for the products and services? What are the ways in which your clients pay you? Will you have a team working to take over the operations of the business? What app or software will you use, if any, to monitor profitability? How will customer communication or support work? These are just the primary things that you will have to decide on.

- Future viability: Try to find out online and by talking to people in the field how long this particular field will last or have a market. Are there new technologies or systems coming up in the near future that would make what you are selling outdated or no longer necessary? Will you be able to continue working the same number of hours as you are now? Without working so long, will you be able to meet your financial and professional targets?

In the next section, I'll be covering some of the main areas that are commonly chosen by self-employed people who are successful at them.

Types of Self-Employment

I have seen this meme floating around once that states, "I'd love to work for myself, if only I could convince myself that it wouldn't be as terrible as working for my boss." Jokes apart, the ultimate question you have to ask yourself is whether self-employment will suit you financially, physically, mentally, and emotionally.

- Affiliate marketing: You can become an agent for existing products and sell them online or via direct sales techniques. If people purchase the product through you, then you will receive a commission. There will be no salary for your role, and your income will be purely based on how much you can sell. You can use your social media handles or blogs to promote the product and post links to it. You can also run banner or poster ads via your personal website.

- Selling products online: You can choose to sell homemade items, craft items, and more on websites such as Amazon, eBay, Etsy, and others. You can also sell items you have purchased from thrift stores on the above sites.

- Dropshipping: This too, involves selling products online. However, there is a slight difference. You work like an agent between the seller and the buyer. You list the seller's products at a slightly higher rate on your e-commerce store. When a buyer purchases the product from you, you alert the seller, who will have it delivered to the buyer. The product doesn't pass through your hands.

- Freelancing: If you are an artist, writer, graphic designer, narrator, or translator, you can sell your services to clients who will pay you for them. Online freelancing has made it infinitely more convenient, and you can work from anywhere you choose. However, to land your initial clients, you will have to have a portfolio of work (preferably published work), set your price, and pitch to them. You can start your own website or blog to market your services and better reach the audience you seek.

- Online tutoring and coaching: It can be a freelance or full-time position. There are companies you can become a part of or start your own coaching academy. You will, of course, have to be an expert in a subject and decide which age group of students you will be teaching. Again, in some cases, you will prepare your own content or syllabus, whereas if you are teaching for an organization, they may provide the content. The actual classes will be conducted via apps such as Zoom or Google Meet. There is a huge demand for tutors in English. You don't need more than a bachelor's degree and a good grasp of the language to help non-speakers pick up the language. Companies like Chegg, Indeed, and others provide online tutoring of this kind. There are platforms such as Coach.me and Clarity.fm where you can sign up as a coach for personal relationships, health and fitness, business, creativity, and even addiction. Since these areas are based on your experience of life, they may not require you to possess an academic or professional degree.

- Creating courses: If you are more of an academic content creator and not so much a real-time teacher,

99

this is an avenue for you to design and create your courses and post them on platforms that will buy them from you and use them for online tutoring. You can use a combination of presentations and videos to record your content and post it on websites such as Teachable and Thinkific. Each time people enroll in your courses and pay for them, you will make money without the hassle of teaching in real-time.

- Creating content and vlogging: YouTube, Instagram, TikTok, and a host of other social media sites allow you to post videos and other educational or entertaining content. Depending on your visibility, you can monetize your content via ads. Additionally, if you can create content for paid promotions, you can increase revenue.

- Selling stock photos: Are you good with the camera, or do you have an eye for detail? You can take photos with your camera and post them on websites such as iStock and Shutterstock. Each time a person licenses your photo, you will earn a couple of dollars. You will have to keep uploading a lot of photos so you can get more hits and make more money. If you can take photos of things and places that are popular and people download them more often, your income will go up.

- Blogging and vlogging: You can start your own site and post content or videos. If it gets popular, you can earn a lot of revenue through affiliate marketing, sponsored posts, selling your line of service, or through ads. You will have to be consistent to gather an audience, but once you get popular, it will be well worth the effort.

- Writing and selling e-books: This field is getting easier but also more competitive. There are an endless number of free resources and ghostwriting services you can employ to write and edit content and then design the cover page. In fact, open AI resources like ChatGPT and others will help you craft the book, from the cover design to the blurb! You can either print this or sell it in eBook format on Amazon and other stores. To promote the book, use your social media handles or your YouTube account.

- Virtual assisting: Though I already mentioned this briefly, let me once again remind you of what an opportunity this is. You can look for these jobs on LinkedIn, Indeed, or Remote.co. Your tasks could include responding to emails and phone calls, making online purchases, managing social media profiles, or sorting data. In short, you will be a personal assistant, just working remotely.

- Doing odd jobs: TaskRabbit will help you monetize your physical skills. For instance, if you are good at repairing electrical and electronic goods, you can search for suitable jobs via the app and then meet a client who wants the laptop repaired and paid for it. If you know basic carpentry, you can choose jobs that require your expertise.

Believe me when I tell you that the list above merely skims the surface of the millions of opportunities available today!

Key Points

- You have to be sure that you want to be self-employed. Worse than a bad boss is that boss being you!

- Identify the market, the opportunities, strengths, and weaknesses. Everything from marketing to distribution will hinge on these.

- Future viability is something you have to seriously consider—how long will I want to and be able to keep doing what I am doing now?

- You have to find out the legal, financial, and other protocols before establishing any trade, online or offline.

- Search, search, search for the work that suits you best. The sky's the limit, but there is also a cap on the number of things you can try out in a lifetime!

- Harking back to a previous section, keep your expectations realistic because even the spectacular success and fame that you see online are the result of months or years of effort. There are only a handful of people who are thrust into fame.

In the next chapter, we will look at some booming job-market trends, which you can further explore.

9

Modernizing Your Arsenal

It is the same with people as it is with riding a bike. Only when moving can one comfortably maintain one's balance. –Albert Einstein

Maciej Malenda and Tomasz Rudolf from Poland were blindsided, like everyone else, when the pandemic struck in 2020. But there was also a flipside. The rise of telemedicine was the perfect answer for people who wanted to be in touch with their doctors, wanted constant surveillance, and yet did not want to physically leave the safety of their homes. Born from their efforts to produce an easy, fast, effective, and remote way of connecting doctors and patients was Doctor.One, launched in 2021. Unlike other apps, this one does not base itself on patient bookings. Doctors can do their rounds with their patients via this app. It is based on a subscription model that allows doctors to check in on their patients, send them prescriptions, reply to patient queries, start a video call (without revealing their personal numbers), and much more. These would help doctors maintain their much-needed work-life balance and yet be available to their patients. Doctor.One has ambitious plans to onboard ten thousand doctors by 2025 and to enter other European markets soon. This one-of-a-kind venture has raised $478,00 in capital to realize its full potential (Allen, 2021).

What likens Maciej and Tomasz to Julius Caesar has a lot to do with the latter's quote: *"veni, vidi, vici"* (I came, I saw, I conquered). They were present when the demand for health surveillance shot up; they saw the problem, and they were willing to do what it took to provide a solution. And that's what

I would beseech of you, dear reader, who has kindly stayed with me on this journey. Here we will explore the newest and latest options available in the job market scenario and how you can make the most of them.

Some Recent Trends

So how do you go about selecting one field that will: Suit you, be there for the long haul, provide you plenty of opportunities, and also satiate your passion? Well, as for passion, that's something you will have to keep your eyes, brain, and heart open. You will have to eventually figure that one out on your own, even if it is with the aid of elimination after a few trials and errors. As for the rest, I can definitely let you in on the secret as to where the world is headed. (Well, it's really no secret; I've just been keeping track of what the experts have been forecasting. It certainly seemed more exciting, to put it that way).

So below are some leads that seem to be opening up promising avenues of work:

- Digitization: Whatever the area, digitization is here to stay. The Internet and technological tools are becoming accessible to more people at a faster pace than ever before. Whether you are looking at law, medicine, science, the arts, business, or any other field, you have to be equipped and skilled to use the latest and best software, apps, and other platforms linked to your field. As I have mentioned before, most good companies no longer seek a degree or certification of your skill. Based on your past experience and projects completed, they will offer you positions. What you need to acquire are skills, not necessarily a degree. Reskilling and upskilling yourself based on the latest developments may be mandatory.

- Artificial intelligence: This area is gaining momentum and is being used in everything from customer support to content creation. It is a brave new world of opportunities that you are entering, as we are yet to discover how AI could alter our futures. Keep track of how it might be shaping your chosen area of work and the latest trends in it. Ask questions to people who are working with AI to find out how AI may be replacing, reshaping, and restructuring the human workforce.

- Mobile workforce: It is estimated that the youngest workers today will hold twelve to fifteen jobs in their lifetime! (Ogunwale, 2022). We are looking at people who are transitioning between jobs and moving from one field to another. So don't be afraid of narrowing down your options to a single profession. In fact, you may actually benefit from having a list of choices with you. This should enable you to look at work as something more fluid than a lifelong nine-to-five association with a single company, unlike some of our parents did.

- Company restructuring: Just as employees are moving, companies are also looking for productivity rather than loyalty from their employees. Thus, just as there have been huge layoffs in the recent past, big companies will be looking to restructure the employee base every time they feel that a vertical is not performing or is becoming redundant. *Layoff* is soon going to lose its ugly connotation and become the norm. And from the success stories that we have heard, being laid off may not be the worst thing to happen to a person, as it would give them the impetus to find another company or vertical where they would be truly valued.

- 5G and cloud computing: 5G is touted as the mother of all communication systems, which will let the entire world converse in a seamless manner. Cloud computing refers to the storage of vast amounts of data on cloud-based systems or rather servers located at several places across the globe. This means that you don't have to carry the data around, and you don't need the infrastructure to store it. You can pay to use the system whenever, wherever, and however you want. The jobs in these areas would be described by terms that you may already come across often: big data, network architecture, machine learning, and the internet of things.

Now that we have a certain basis for predicting hiring models and fields that could witness a boom in the next couple of years, let us look at a specific way in which you can prepare to become a part of these.

Online Marketplaces and How They Pay

Every one of us has some marketable skill or another. Yes, even you, who are just a student trying to get by in college or working your way into college, will have something that you can sell. And a primary search will mostly reveal that your skill will be marketable online. At this point, I'm not talking about technical skills like coding that you may excel at. I'm talking of everyday skills that you may possess to make things, paint, write, or even doodle. And what better time than now to enter the job market? You don't even have to get yourself hired! You can simply choose an online market and put your products up for sale there. If they sell, great. If not, just try again until you find something you can make that sells.

Why am I pushing you to do this? One is the money that you can make. But two, and this is more important as far as I'm concerned, is the experience and confidence that doing this will give you. So, when I talk about *pay*, I'm not merely talking of the monetary benefit that this could bring you. All the trends we listed above are happening within online marketing, so why wouldn't it be a great place to be?

The following are some advantages of being an online seller:

- Reduced setting up cost: There isn't any infrastructure or logistics that you need to be worried about. The cost of setting up your store will be negligible as compared to setting up a physical store.

- The flexibility of workspace: You can work from home or from any part of the globe (in your PJs on your bed or in your bathing suit on the beach) where the online market operates. You don't have to be available at one particular location.

- Greater market reach and visibility: With a physical store, there is only a localized community that you can reach. An online store can bring you global customers, if you market it right.

- Constant monitoring and scalability: You can monitor your sales and costs, as well as review which products are doing well and which aren't. Based on this data, you can scale up or down your business in the future. Apart from this, online marketplaces will also give you live tracking of the shipment and delivery of your products.

- 24/7 business: Unlike a regular shop, which has to close down, an online business is open all day and through the week, and customers can place orders at any time, which will allow more productive hours of sales for you.

- **Larger profits:** Since you do not spend money on paying rent or dealing with the other costs of maintaining a physical store, your profits could be larger.

Now that we have looked at why setting up shop virtually has its share of benefits, let us quickly run through some of the best-ranked online marketplaces that most people would vouch for in terms of seller–buyer satisfaction. The following are platforms available all over the world: Apart from these; there are local platforms that have a strong presence in certain regions, like Shopee in Southeast Asia or Flipkart in India, which you can explore.

- Amazon
- eBay
- AliExpress (Alibaba group)
- Rakuten
- Etsy

Depending on what you are selling, you will have to make a list of the pros and cons of each of the above platforms. For instance, Etsy is more popular than Amazon when it comes to craft items and handmade home decor. Amazon has a huge presence but is intensely competitive and charges a selling fee. Ultimately, you have to decide which platform works best for you and the kind of products you wish to sell.

A Step-by-Step Guide

Still confused and hazy about the whole process? Well, you can just follow the steps below to become your own boss. (Ahh! The freedom and sweetness those words bring!)

1. Determine the kind of item(s) that you want to sell. This has to be something you are good at and in which you know you have enduring patience and interest. If you aren't particularly creative, you can think of purchasing or sourcing items from local stores and then putting them up online as well.

2. Check out online marketplaces that are reliable and listed by most sellers as being safe in terms of payments and where the chances of falling prey to scams are lesser. Remember to do your homework as early and efficiently as possible. Also, remember to compare and contrast the pros and cons of the platforms you are looking at.

3. Develop your skills. Think of ways you can market your store and goods. Will you use social media? Would you want to use your personal accounts, or will you create a separate account for your business on social media platforms? Can you get your peers or friends to give some publicity to your venture? Get creative and talk to as many people as you can.

4. Start bidding and proposing to offer services. Remember, the competition out there is tough. What more can you bring to the table for a buyer that would make them choose you over other sellers who are putting up the same or similar products? Cost is an essential marker of the difference between you and your competitor. However, if you can provide better quality

or better customer service, perhaps the price differential can be justified.

5. Reputation is everything. Get customers to leave feedback and build up a positive rapport with repeat buyers. When you get negative feedback, analyze what you can do better and where you can improve.

6. Once you do get a steady stream of clients, you can think about setting up a dedicated website of your own, from which customers can directly place their orders. You won't have to depend on an intermediary platform anymore. You can exercise more control over your products and sales. As your sales volume grows, you can think about outsourcing options. Certain parts of the work you do can be handled by others on your payroll. For instance, perhaps the management of social media or the logistics can be handled by a separate team. Eventually, as your business grows, you can think of unique ways to promote it, like writing a book on your entrepreneurial journey or how you grew your business, etc. You can also think of podcasting or conducting talks for youngsters who are interested in starting a business venture of their own, etc.

Do you know what is another one of my favorite words? *Trajectory*. Once you start something of your own, you can carve out your own trajectory and branch off in directions that you had never thought of earlier. It also gives you the freedom to choose what you want to do next. This will not just make you a richer person in terms of the money you accumulate but also add to your personal experience account.

Take it from me: When you work towards money, it can be the hardest thing to come by. Work towards a passion, and money will come chasing you. Your focus will be so totally on conquering more personal and professional milestones that money will be the least of your concerns. Hard to digest? Well, I promise it's only the truth.

Key Points

- Not all opportunities come knocking at your door; perhaps it is time you create opportunities for yourself. Register yourself as a seller on an online marketplace and give it a try. It will build your confidence immensely and enrich your resume.

- Consider aspects such as competition, selling fee, target market, and market reach when you decide on the platform.

- Use marketing and customer interaction to build your reputation.

- Think of ways to expand by creating your own website and platform.

In the last (but not least) section of this book, we will look at some final qualities and a tricky term called "personal branding" before we wind up.

10

Vanquishing Vulnerability

In matters of principle, stand like a rock; in matters of style, swim with the current. –Unknown.

I'm sure a lot of you have heard of this very famous moral story, "A Pound of Butter." If you haven't, let me quickly narrate it for you:

There was a baker who always used to buy a pound of butter from a farmer. One day he wanted to verify the weight of the butter he was receiving. He weighed it on his scale and was furious when he found out that he was being short-changed. The butter he got was less than a pound. He was upset, thinking he had been made a fool of for such a long time. Needless to say, he took the farmer to court. The judge asked the farmer, "Do you hear the allegation? How do you measure your butter, man?" The farmer replied, "Sir, it's true. I am a poor man and have only a rudimentary scale to measure my butter. But I always weighed the butter I gave him with the pound of bread he gave me every morning!" The judge looked at the baker, who was by now hanging his head in shame (Swart, 2019).

I don't have to provide you with a moral to this story. *As you sow, so shall you reap* is an adage all of you must be familiar with. Never mind if you aren't, for you will definitely know another saying made famous by Justin Timberlake's song, "What goes around, comes around." What I am hinting at is that what you practice in your personal and professional lives will come back to you. Keep going in good faith, and no, good people don't necessarily have to finish last!

One of my personal mottos in life is to be kind, as far as possible, to as many people as I can. In my general observation, kindness is gravely underestimated in the professional sphere. Kindness is usually seen as a flaw, a weakness, or, at best, an indulgence. However, I will go as far as to say that being kind can be a strength. This is not to say that you shouldn't draw limits or that you should be the ever-generous giving tree, reduced to a stump by people who are never tired of taking from you and who never give you anything in return. However, I do believe that kindness can set in motion a chain reaction of similar actions, which can make people stronger as a unit and happier working together. Being happy where you are and at what you do is half the battle won, at least in my opinion.

This final chapter of the book will look at some important values that you can contemplate, which will help you build the mental strength, courage, and integrity to live your dreams, despite the many challenges that you may meet.

Introspection

I know I have talked about this at least twice already in the course of this book. But here I am going to elaborate on this concept and give you a list of questions, which, if you answer them honestly, will be the compass for your direction in life. But before we proceed, I would like to also segregate this part into two sections: The first is related to personal introspection, and the other is related to professional goals.

Personal Introspection

In human psychology, our personalities are generally divided into five broad categories. This is only a starting point, a sort of primary framework that uses human responses to situations to determine a personality type. Now, let me stress here that these personality types need not be mutually exclusive, and you may find yourself possessing characteristics of more than one personality type.

There have also been numerous studies conducted that suggest that adolescence and even young adulthood (some say even up to the age of 25) are an age where the human brain and one's psychological tendencies are still developing. So, please do not feel pressured to classify and pigeonhole yourself into any one of the categories below.

The following should serve to educate more than anything else.

1. The neurotic: (I'm not quite sure why this is always the first character to be listed on most sites, but I'm going with the tradition.) This personality trait is generally termed negative, and a person belonging to this category won't be able to exercise control over his moods. They will be moody, irritable, and emotionally unstable.

2. The extravert: A person who is gregarious, outgoing, bold, and assertive, an extravert is generally seen as an asset to any organization. Extraversion is normally considered a desirable personality trait. However, there are also counterclaims as to how extraversion can become a cry for attention.

3. The intellectual (or the inquisitive one): These are people who are curious and open to exploring more about things, are creative, and are most academically

gifted. They are quick to learn things and love to experiment with the data and facts given to them.

4. The agreeable one: Possessing empathy and kindness, an agreeable person tries their best to offer support to others and, in turn, is usually compliant and modest. Conversely, they sometimes turn so agreeable as to internalize their personal problems and carry around the baggage of their sufferings.

5. The conscientious one: This includes a hard-working, law-abiding person who is controlled and cautious in their interactions with others. They could be achievers in their own right and will probably live long, healthy lives (Grice, 2019).

As I'm not a certified psychologist, I won't be going in-depth here about the five traits, as I'm betting you, as a reader, are smart enough to do that for yourself, should you feel the need to look them up.

Instead, I'll pose a few questions to which you can respond in your spare time. Ideally, I would ask you to take a diary and divide its pages into ten parts, with each of the questions below starting a new section. Alternatively, you can maintain an online diary or even a Google Doc. Feel free to revisit these questions over time and reframe or clarify your answers whenever you feel the need for them.

You may also find that some of your priorities will change with time, and that's okay too.

1. How would I describe myself?

2. What are my goals in life? (a) Short-term goals, and (b) Long-term goals

3. The things I am grateful for are: (List as many as you want to.)

4. The things I love doing best, ranked in order of best to least, are:

5. What are my fears?

6. What are my core values? (List the top four here.)

7. Describe one instance (an achievement or an incident) where I'm proud of myself. Why am I proud of this?

8. Describe an instance (a failure or an incident) where I wasn't proud of myself. What could I have done better or instead?

9. What aspects of my nature should I work on improving?

10. How do I plan on implementing these improvements in my nature?

These questions will provide you with some answers that will prove much more useful than trying to reduce yourself to one of five personality types. To use business terminology, you can choose to be "the sum of your parts" or not!

Personal to Professional Branding

Personal branding sounds very businesslike, almost as if your sole purpose in life were to sell your ideas, your vision, or yourself for gain (Ugh! That doesn't sound nice one bit!). But it isn't as materialistic as it sounds. Personal branding is an exercise in identifying and working towards your unique potential and becoming the best version of yourself. Now you can hardly dispute that, can you? A professional branding is how you use your uniqueness to meet your and your company's objectives.

In the section below, I have tried to list out some of the most common problems that young adults face and what they can do to get out of their ruts.

Some Common Barriers and Coping Strategies

As a teenager or young adult, some of the challenges you would face can be summed up as follows:

- Intellectual: You do not think you are smart enough or intelligent enough to fit into an academic course or group. Maybe you often feel that academic exams and skills don't measure your true worth. Sometimes you are upset that you are not able to do justice to things you have to study or learn.

- Physical: You feel stressed, tired, or sleepy all the time. You feel that you aren't as healthy as some of your peers. Early signs of sleeplessness could also start during these years.

- Emotional: Suddenly, you might be exposed to a variety of emotions, including sadness, anxiety, depression, anger, guilt, jealousy, and fear. These can be owing to a variety of reasons encompassing intellectual and social pressures.

- Social: This can be related to not fitting in with social groups or changing dynamics with family members and the resulting stress. It can be due to the pressures of being in or not being in a romantic relationship.

- Spiritual: Young adulthood is also a time when your beliefs, faith, and other values may be questioned, and you may start doubting them and even changing your opinions about a few of them. This, too, can result in emotional and intellectual anxiety.

Now that we have identified the barriers, the logical question would be, "How do we deal with them?" I would list three strategies:

- Letting go: I will be talking about perseverance in a while. However, if after giving something (a pursuit, vocation, profession, or even a relationship) your best shot, it still does not work out despite multiple attempts; then perhaps it's time to accept that this is probably not your true calling. There have been innumerable successful people who started out on a different track and found their true path much later.

- Taking disappointments and failures in stride: You can achieve nothing without taking risks. When you take risks, some of these will yield results, and others won't. You have to accept failure and disappointment as friends who will visit you from time to time. Embracing failure for failure, is part of the road to success. Instead of focusing on your failure, you have to pay attention to where you can improve so that the next time you try, your chances of success are that much better.

- Tackling self-doubt: It is okay to be apprehensive about one's worth. This is natural for all human beings. Self-doubt sometimes propels you into putting in more effort. But if it prevents you from taking any action and cripples your motivation to do anything, then it has to be nipped in the bud. Think of positive traits and feedback received that will restore your faith in yourself.

The above strategies are mostly responses to problems like stress. Let me go one step further and talk about what you can do actively to start building your brand. Below are some concrete steps that you can implement in most aspects of your life.

- Create a game plan: Always plan. I'm not saying everything will work out according to plan. Having a plan will give you the confidence that comes from being prepared. Changing or modifying an existing plan could be easier than always building one from scratch for every new situation that you face.

- Take charge: Be proactive and find out things to do, places to go, and people to meet. There are very few opportunities that fall into your lap. For the rest, you will have to go searching or make the right connections. As the great actor and comedian Milton Berle once said, "If opportunity doesn't knock, build a door."

- Connect: Man was designed to be a social animal. I cannot emphasize the importance of building the right contacts enough, whether they are teachers, counselors, peers, or your parents. Establish a wide and varied network of people you can turn to for help and guidance and whom you can help too. People are attracted to others belonging to the same social, intellectual, and economic backgrounds. But break the norm and make friends from different ages, ethnicities, and backgrounds.

- Persist: Persevere in your goals. Most people who have become successful have tried hard and failed many times to get where they are. Just because you don't always see the effort that goes into something doesn't mean that it doesn't exist. Also, remember that what you try for with your heart, soul, and body becomes all the sweeter when you actually achieve it.

Next, let us look into something you would term your ethics or your core values.

Core Values

Core values can include many aspects that make up your being. But for ease of explanation, let me segregate this into a few easily digestible topics.

- Personal qualities: Remember the ten questions we answered in the previous section? These will go towards determining some of your personal qualities. Remember that, like your personality category, your personal qualities can also be subjective. A person who is generally good can make a bad mistake at times, right? But overall, these are the qualities you would use to describe yourself. Some examples could be: bold, talkative, friendly, reserved, intellectual, fun-loving, introspective, impulsive, etc. Think of as many adjectives as you possibly can.

- Importance: Think about why you are important or unique. This could be a shorter list, picking out those qualities or combinations of qualities that make you stand out. For instance, you could be impulsive and a good decision-maker most of the time. You might have sensed that you make quick choices, not exactly based on prior planning, but most of the time, your decisions turn out to be well-timed or accurate. In other words, you may have to rebrand yourself as having a good gut instinct rather than as being impulsive. See what I'm doing? A lot of times, what you consider your weakness could even be your hidden strength.

- Values: These are the things you believe in. This could be a long list, but try to number them in order of their priority to you. For instance, my list would run something like: family, health, work, love, education, contentment, commitment, etc. Yours doesn't have to follow that particular order and may contain items that I don't value personally. The purpose of this list is to identify what you can't do without in life, what you can negotiate on, and what you can absolutely neglect.

- A sense of purpose: What gives you a sense of being in life? Is it growth in terms of learning that makes you happy? Do you want to be financially successful? Is it a combination of both? Maybe you want to help people, and that's how you find your purpose. Your sense of purpose is what brings you the most joy and meaning in your life. If you can find this, then the confusion of what you must do next becomes a much easier hurdle.

As you move from qualities to purpose, you will also find the key to how you want to brand yourself. You will learn ways to turn your weaknesses into strengths and capitalize on your strengths.

A Few Resources

The following are a couple of resources that would augment your understanding of career choices and which I am sure you would like to sample as you proceed on your journey. Some of them were funny, others honest, but all of them were inspiring, and we know all of us could use a little of that most days, eh?

Websites and e–Resources

- The Heroic Journey of Teenagers by Gordon Barnhart: A website that offers a lot of ideas to start your journey towards self-fulfillment.

- CareerVillage: A place you can sign up and ask questions regarding specific careers for teens and college-going students.

- A Day in the Life by Firsthand: Thousands of professionals have written articles about a day from their professional life and what their job involves.

- Job Shadowing: Hundreds of interviews with different working professionals explaining their roles and how their day looks.

Key Points

- To have a better understanding of yourself, start with the personal.

- Slowly start looking for the unique among your personal qualities.

- How would you rebrand your weaknesses as your strengths?

- What are your core values, in order of their priority to you?

- What are the things that give you a sense of purpose?

- To face challenges: Learn to embrace failures, be proactive, connect with people, and above all, persist. If everything fails, look around and change track.

Conclusion

I feel I should end with a story, don't you? So here goes.

There was once a king who wanted his fortune told. So he sent out an edict inviting soothsayers from all over the land to predict what would happen to him. So a motley crowd of fortune tellers, diviners, and clairvoyants congregated in the castle. The emperor called them forward. He told them, "I am a busy man. But I want to hear all your predictions. I beseech you to come forward, one person at a time, a day at a time, to tell me what is in store for me."

The first fellow said, "Oh, King. You will live a long and fruitful life. Your reign, I see, will be peaceful, and your subjects will love you. However, you will witness the death of many of your kinsmen in this life."

The king was angered by this last statement. He said, "Stupid seer! Throw him into the dungeons for this horrible prediction!"

The next day, another psychic stepped forward. He too, delivered pretty much the same news as his predecessor, but paused before giving the last bit of news.

"Anything more?" The king asked impatiently.

"Well. As my esteemed colleague said yesterday, I too, see all your relatives dying before you."

"Fool!" The king cried in rage. "Have him tossed into the dungeons as well."

On the third day, a wise old sayer stepped forward, and while the rest of his predictions remained constant, he said, "Kind king, I see that you will outlive many of your kinsmen and live to see your great-grandchildren."

The king now beamed at the soothsayer and rewarded him (*Akbar's Dream—Akbar Birbal Stories for Kids*, 2017).

This story pretty much sums up what this book has been trying to tell you. All three men had the same resources at their disposal, but only one succeeded. The last man did what the others did not—that is, he thought of an out-of-the-box way to solve the problem at hand. And this made all the difference.

As a last word, I hope that you have had fun reading this book. *Choosing a Career Path for Teens* has been the work of a lifetime of searching for answers to questions that had me burning as a teenager, trying to find my way through the bewildering tangle of careers, professions, and jobs. I certainly hope that having read this book has made your path a little easier. I wish you all the best, whether your dream is to become an astronaut, artist, or accountant! Bon voyage!

References

A Day in the Life. (n.d.). Firsthand.co. https://firsthand.co/library/collections/a-day-in-the-life

A Panchatantra Story of the Three Fish for Kids. (2023, January 24). Vedantu. https://www.vedantu.com/stories/three-fish-story-for-kids

About Sophia Amoruso. (2020). Sophia Amoruso. https://www.sophiaamoruso.com/about

About Us. (2023). Buttonsmith Inc. https://www.buttonsmith.com/pages/about-us

Akbar's Dream - Akbar Birbal Stories for Kids. (2017, April 5). Mocomi Kids. https://mocomi.com/akbars-dream/

Allen, P. (2021, December 2). *Warsaw-based startup Doctor.One raises €440k to build a European healthcare network.* EU-Startups. https://www.eu-startups.com/2021/12/warsaw-based-startup-doctor-one-raises-e440k-to-build-a-european-healthcare-network/

Barnhart, G. (2019). *Your Sense of Purpose.* The Heroic Journey of Teenagers. https://teenheroicjourney.org/book/3-core-challenges/forming-an-identity/your-identity-puzzle/your-purpose/

Belasco, A., Bergman, D., & Trivette, M. (2020). Colleges Worth Your Money: A Guide to What America's Top Schools Can Do for You. Rowman & Littlefield.

Being your own boss is great, you get to choose which 18 hours a day you work. (n.d.). Pinterest. https://in.pinterest.com/pin/130956301641463610/

Career A-Z list. (2015, November 26). Nidirect. https://www.nidirect.gov.uk/services/career-z-list

Career Planning for Teens. (2021, October 27). HealthHub. https://www.healthhub.sg/a-z/support-groups-and-others/23/early-career-planning-for-teens-ehb

CareerVillage. (n.d.). Careervillage.org. https://www.careervillage.org/

Carroll, L. (2016). Chapter II: The Pool of Tears. *Alice's Adventures in Wonderland.* Gutenberg. https://www.gutenberg.org/files/11/11-h/11-h.htm

Clinton, H. R. (n.d.). *Quotable Quote.* Goodreads. https://www.goodreads.com/quotes/659277-don-t-confuse-having-a-career-with-having-a-life

Cook, N., & National Journal. (2014, May 14). Is 8th Grade Too Early to Pick a Career? The Atlantic; The Atlantic. https://www.theatlantic.com/business/archive/2014/05/is-8th-grade-too-early-to-pick-a-career/426099/

Dautaj, J., & Meleen, M. (2018, December 12). *Career Planning for Teens.* LoveToKnow. https://teens.lovetoknow.com/Career_Planning_for_Teens

Definition of *Career.* (n.d.). Merriam-Webster. https://www.merriam-webster.com/dictionary/career

Definition of *Self-employment.* (n.d.). Merriam-Webster. https://www.merriam-webster.com/dictionary/self-employment

Edmunds, W. (2022, December 5). *Is There a Doctor in the House?*. 3 Seas Europe. https://3seaseurope.com/doctor-one-doctorone-polish-startup-medical/

Encourage Your Teens to Explore Career Options. (n.d.). Alis-Alberta. https://alis.alberta.ca/tools-and-resources/resources-for-parents/resources-for-parents-help-your-children-plan-their-careers/encourage-your-teens-to-explore-career-options/

Explore your Career Options by shadowing real jobs online. (n.d.). Job Shadow. https://jobshadow.com/

Federal Student Aid. (n.d.). Studentaid.gov. https://studentaid.gov/understand-aid/eligibility/requirements

Fiske Guide to Colleges 2023 (39th). (2022). Sourcebooks.

From N40,000 to a Multimillion Dollar Business! Abasiama Idaresit is Transforming the Digital Marketing Space in Africa #BellaNaijaMCM. (2017, January 23). BellaNaija. https://www.bellanaija.com/2017/01/from-n40000-to-a-multimillion-dollar-business-abasiama-idaresit-is-transforming-the-digital-marketing-space-in-africa-bellanaijamcm/

Global trends that will impact careers in 2023. (2023, January 4). India Today. https://www.indiatoday.in/education-today/featurephilia/story/global-trends-that-will-impact-careers-in-2023-2317091-2023-01-04

Grice, J. W. (2019). Five-factor model of personality. *Encyclopædia Britannica*. https://www.britannica.com/science/five-factor-model-of-personality

Harris, N. (2022, June 6). *18 Back-to-School Quotes to Get Kids Excited for Class*. Parents. https://www.parents.com/kids/education/back-to-school/back-to-school-quotes-to-get-kids-excited-for-class/

High School Classes Colleges Look For. (n.d.). BigFuture—College Board. https://bigfuture.collegeboard.org/plan-for-college/college-prep/thrive-in-high-school/high-school-classes-colleges-look-for

How to choose a career path as a teenager. (2022, October 26). Spikeview. https://www.spikeview.com/advice-for-teens-choosing-career-path/

Huff, E. (2011, June 8). *In matters of style, swim with the current...(Spurious Quotation)*. Monticello. https://www.monticello.org/research-education/thomas-jefferson-encyclopedia/matters-style-swim-currentspurious-quotation/

Lafferty, T. (2020). *Be More Like You: A Guide to Answering the Ultimate Question "What do I want to do with my life?"*. Tyler Lafferty.

Lees, J. (2016). *How to get a job you'll love*. Mcgraw-Hill Education.

Life Is Like Riding a Bicycle. To Keep Your Balance You Must Keep Moving. (2015, June 29). Quoteinvestigator.com. https://quoteinvestigator.com/2015/06/28/bicycle/

Liz Smith Quotes. (n.d.). Quotes.net. https://www.quotes.net/quote/17582.

Lore, N. (2008). *Now What? The Young Person's Guide to Choosing the Perfect Career*. Simon and Schuster.

Mariana Costa Checa - Co-Founder/CEO at Laboratoria. (2022, May 11). Rest of World. https://restofworld.org/profile/mariana-costa-checa/

Melanie Perkins. (n.d.). Forbes. https://www.forbes.com/profile/melanie-perkins/?sh=3bf659371265

Mileva, G. (2023, January 4). *The 15 Best Online Marketplaces for E-Commerce Brands and Sellers.* Influencer Marketing Hub. https://influencermarketinghub.com/online-marketplaces/

Murakami, H. (n.d.). *Quotable Quote.* Goodreads. https://www.goodreads.com/quotes/168421-the-most-important-thing-we-learn-at-school-is-the

Ogunwale, S. (2022, September 9). *Five key trends that are shaping the new world of work.* World Economic Forum. https://www.weforum.org/agenda/2022/09/five-trends-endure-world-of-work/

PaySimple. (2018, July 10). *How to Become Self-Employed: 10 Steps for Taking the Plunge.* PaySimple Blog. https://paysimple.com/blog/how-to-become-self-employed-10-steps-for-taking-the-plunge/

Penn, M. (2016). *You got this! : unleash your awesomeness, find your path, and change your world.* North Star Way.

Shakespeare, W. (n.d.). Act II Scene 5. *Twelfth Night Or, What You Will* (p. 85). In B. A. Mowat & P. Werstine (Eds.), Folger Shakespeare Library. https://shakespeare.folger.edu/downloads/pdf/twelfth-night_PDF_FolgerShakespeare.pdf

Smale, W. (2013, September 29). Young woman breaks through in Sri Lankan business world. *BBC News.* https://www.bbc.com/news/business-24206038

Srinivasan, S. (2022, October 21). *15 Employment Trends In 2021 Shaping The Future Of Jobs.* Feedough. https://www.feedough.com/employment-trends-2019/

Strong, J. (1901). *The Times and Young Men.* Google Books (p. 124). Baker and Taylor. https://books.google.co.in/books?id=VUYNxK7rYsAC&q=sharpening&redir_esc=y&hl=en#v=snippet&q=sharpening&f=false

Swart, L. (2019, September 1). *From the short stories series: A Pound of Butter.* Lisanne Swart. https://www.lisanneswart.com/2019/09/01/from-the-short-stories-series-a-pound-of-butter/

Take Your High School Classes to the Next Level. (n.d.). BigFuture; College Board. https://bigfuture.collegeboard.org/plan-for-college/college-prep/thrive-in-high-school/how-to-take-your-high-school-classes-to-the-next-level

Tauszik, K. (2020). *When I Graduate, I Want To Be...: The 10-Step Career Planning Journal.* Tip Top Books.

Teens' Guide to College and Career Planning (2022). Peterson's.

Types of Colleges: The Basics. (n.d.). BigFuture—College Board. https://bigfuture.collegeboard.org/plan-for-college/college-basics/types-of-colleges/types-of-colleges-the-basics

The Complete Book of Colleges, 2021: The Mega-Guide to 1,349 Colleges and Universities. (2020). Princeton Review.

The US Higher Education System Explained. (2022, November 10). Shorelight. https://shorelight.com/student-stories/the-us-higher-education-system-explained/

Understanding the American Education System. (2021, November 7). Study in the USA. https://www.studyusa.com/en/a/58/understanding-the-american-education-system

Vadhera, K. (2020, December 11). *8 Major Advantages of Starting Online Marketplace for Local Businesses*. JungleWorks. https://jungleworks.com/8-major-advantages-of-starting-online-marketplace-for-local-businesses/

Williams, T. (2022, November 17). The stories behind the most successful Australian entrepreneurs - UTS Open. Open.uts.edu.au. https://open.uts.edu.au/insights/success-stories/most-successful-australian-entrepreneurs/#:~:text=Ruslan%20Kogan%20%2D%20Kogan.com

Image References

Lynch, O. (2018). *Resume*. Pixabay. https://pixabay.com/photos/cv-resume-job-employment-business-3726428/

Made in the USA
Las Vegas, NV
21 April 2025